Global Transition

Our Path Into The Future

Stuart Price

ISBN: 9798874071387
Published by KS Creative Arts, Ingol, Preston, UK
First Edition 2024

"The world as we have created it is a process of our thinking. It cannot be changed without changing our thinking." - Albert Einstein

Introduction

The coronavirus pandemic of 2019-2020 created a massive global shock to the way we all live and work, resulting in a pause to normal operations of our entire political, economic, education, health and social systems. It brought into sharp perspective a whole range of issues concerning the relationship between ordinary people and the "powers that be"; many of which had been brewing beneath the surface for a while and that emerged into general view with the opportunity created by covid.

Some people were forced into working from home rather than engage in a stressful daily commute through increasingly gridlocked roads. The prevalence of computer-based working made this easily possible for considerable numbers and has heralded a workstyle change that has proved very popular with many. As well as individual benefits to the worker, the massive reduction in traffic created an immediate improvement in both air and noise pollution; with noticeable subsequent health benefits. For a significant number, working from home has led to a long-term preference for this lifestyle, with multiple advantages in terms of work-life balance, childcare duties and a general improvement in perceived well-being. However, it has also brought out a new area of conflict with employers and reignited ancient controversies about laziness and skiving off.

The restrictions placed upon travel and association with others also opened up a national debate about individual rights and freedoms and the way that these were coming into conflict with government-imposed restrictions based, in this case, on public health concerns. The mood around this was soured somewhat by media aired disagreements between politicians and health professionals; framed around a conflict of values concerning whether the health of the economy or the health of people was the most important factor. To add to this, a considerable number of people subscribed to conspiracy theories claiming that the whole covid phenomenon was a scam and a fiction, while others, perhaps more accurately, drew comparisons with our general mistreatment of the natural world making the appearance of pandemics more likely. For too many, the disease brought immense suffering, isolation and painful deaths.

To summarize all the issues, the general view was that coronavirus was a bad thing and the best outcome was to get back to normal as soon as possible. However not everyone thought like this. For many, the pandemic brought a relief from the daily grind and the opportunity to experience new sensations. For too many people, normal daily life is experienced as increasingly stressful & troubling; anxiety, fear and depression becoming ever more common. With lockdown commencing, many suddenly found themselves entering into a new relationship with the natural world. As the incessant racket of traffic noise ceased, a new soundscape entered awareness; undulating breeze, the rustle of leaves in the trees and birdsong became the new normal and was found to be good. Many became aware, possibly for the first time, of the sheer beauty of nature all around us and its positive effect on our well-being. For others, the restrictions on work and association opened up an opportunity to re-consider what they really wanted to do with their life. There was a sense that, despite the obvious financial, social & emotional difficulties that covid brought, perhaps we are meant to live at a slower, more mindful and more meaningful pace. Do we really want to go back to what we are led to believe is "normal"?

Normal, for many in poor countries, is a daily battle just to survive. And it's not just them. Increasingly, the news reports the latest extreme weather event and environmental catastrophe to blight a community. Across the UK, flooding events routinely described as "once in every 100 years frequency" are becoming regular and common. Nature is in catastrophic decline with the United Nations describing up to a million species at risk of extinction. Air pollution, traffic congestion and the resultant impact on our health, is getting worse. Political corruption, manipulation &

cronyism is visible for all to see. The life of our rivers, streams and seas is being poisoned by human faeces... as well as a vast tidal wave of filth: chemicals, plastics and industrial pollution.

Furthermore, the vast army of workers whose survival depends on creating an income within the political & economic system producing all this, is finding it increasingly difficult to keep going. Mental health difficulties caused by modern life have been described as an "epidemic" of stress, depression and anxiety. One study[1] revealed that 60%, that's a clear majority, of working professionals experience at least mild symptoms of anxiety, and 1 in 4 meet the threshold for clinically relevant symptoms of mental health disorders. The health system is unable to cope with all this. For those who do manage to soldier on, it is with growing awareness that some are still not making enough to pay for housing, food and energy, even with 2nd or 3rd jobs. Businesses are also struggling, as costs & bureaucracy escalate out of sustainability. At the same time, the wealth, power and privilege of a tiny global financial elite, those who determine the course of our economic and political systems, is increasing at an accelerating rate. Our whole society appears to be moving into a very disturbed and disturbing phase; harmful both to human beings and the natural world of which we are an integral

---

1. From "Champion Health: How to spot mental health issues at work". <championhealth.co.uk>

part. In summation, these issues and many, many more, constitute what can be termed a "whole system crisis".

Today, Friday September 8th 2023, hidden within the normal & regular news items of how many have died in the latest "biblical" downpour of rain, not to mention the increasing number of violent wars blighting innocent civilians, the United Nations published in draft form the basis of the first "global stocktake" under the 2015 Paris agreement to tackle climate change. That process is meant to track countries' efforts to meet the goals of the treaty. While basically repeating the fact that global leaders are not doing what is needed, despite the required knowledge, means and money existing, the report includes the line: "Achieving net zero CO_2 and greenhouse gas emissions requires systems transformation across all sectors and contexts." To repeat, **ALL** sectors and contexts. In other words, the entire social, political & economic system.

Our present societal system, built upon what came before and determining the way we live, work and learn, is based on a series of historical transitions, periods of major & significant change, that have regularly taken place since the time that human beings first appeared on this planet. Most recently, it is based on the framework of core ideas that guided the development of the last major transition of the 18th Century Industrial Revolution; the time from when the atmospheric build-up of fossil fuel emissions began. These ideas constitute the foundations of our current politics, economics, education, science, technology, religion, trade, transport, work patterns & relationships to name but a few, although built upon the principles of much earlier civilisations. They can be thought of as a "story" or narrative that governs our thinking in these areas. They are what society currently regards as normal. They are not inevitable, and they are beginning to change as the old story collapses and the current societal system becomes increasingly dysfunctional and unable to effectively resolve the many crises we face.

This book outlines the main features of the story, how it came into being and how it is related to the whole system crisis into which we are sinking. The story has undoubtedly brought us multiple benefits, including a widespread relative affluence and the way that we are now an integrated world community, with a planetary real-time communications system accessible to most. However, it has also brought us to a point where our entire global society is now possibly in danger of collapse from climate change, environmental destruction, economic crises, escalating warfare and a way of life that is harming both ourselves and the natural world of which we are an interdependent part. Within nature, as well as human societies, such radical crises often occur and precede major ecological change and evolutionary adjustment to a new condition of harmony and well-being.

The book details those changes as they occurred in the past and are occurring now. Beginning in the 20th century, a new story of new ideas began to emerge, which signposts a new direction to reverse the current destructive trend. It's natural to fear change and to try and hang on to the known & familiar. However, the change that is now taking place has its best elements within the hearts and minds of intelligent people of goodwill; those from all cultures and backgrounds who believe that a more beautiful world is possible and needed. The book deals with vast themes, many skimmed over, as well as possibly missing out lots of relevant issues. As you read it, you will doubtless come up with your own ideas: "but what about...?". This is part of the process. It's not about someone telling you how it is. Rather its designed to act as a catalyst to your own insights; your own part of the jigsaw puzzle that we're all trying to make sense of and that is collectively arising "from the bottom up" within countless millions of us. We all have a different and unique perspective on the changes taking place and that need to take place. We all have our own unique role to play in the planetary drama that is now being enacted.

This is the global transition.

Contents

Chapter 1. Transitions within Human History　p15

Chapter 2. The Industrial Revolution　p38

Chapter 3. Economics & Finance　p61

Chapter 4. Politics & Governance　p85

Chapter 5. Science: Entry into a New Reality　p109

Chapter 6. The 20th Century Enlightenment　p129

Chapter 7. Mother Earth; Jewel of the Cosmos　p155

Chapter 1

Transitions in Human History[2]

The overall theme of this book is that humanity as a whole is currently within a historical period of transition from one type of society into something very different. A major rationale for this viewpoint, apart from the fact that vast numbers of people recognise how urgently it's now needed, is that it's happened many times before. Although the nature of human society, its norms, expectations and ways of life, has been a continuously unfolding process over long aeons, with hindsight it's possible to recognise distinct moments of major change. We can look back over history and identify key periods where something very radical happened that has had an enduring influence over the way we live today.

---

2. The transitional model in this chapter is taken from "The Major Transitions in the History of Human Transformation of the Biosphere" by András Takács-Sánta, Hungarian Academy of Sciences and Eötvös University Research Group for Evolutionary Genetics and Molecular Genetics, Eötvös Loránd University of Sciences, Pázmány Péter sétány 1/C, 1117 Budapest, HUNGARY. The model is based on research by Holdren and Ehrlich (1974), who define "transitions" as governed by three principle factors: population size, effect on the biosphere and economic activity.

From our twenty first century perspective they can be identified as profoundly significant, marking an enduring difference with what went before and directly contributing to the present state of human civilisation. These moments were not necessarily immediate, perhaps taking place over tens, hundreds or thousands of years. However, it can be discerned that the frequency of such changes, the impact they have had and the speed at which they take place increases the nearer we move to the present day. For this reason, many people regard the current transitional period as the most important and significant one of them all.

Before identifying these transitional moments, there are several major issues of concern with any analysis of history. Firstly, the further back we look, our understanding of what exactly took place is dependent upon archaeological remains; physical evidence of the way that people lived then. The further back we look, especially before written records, the less evidence there is and the more we rely on our interpretation of that evidence. That interpretation is necessarily made through the lens of a modern-day psychology and mindset. It's tempting to assume, and many do so, that our current ways of thinking are more advanced than those of the past. Humans of pre-history are judged to be in some way more "primitive" & less developed than us. Actually, that way of thinking, as we will shortly discuss, is a product one of the transitions in our model.

A second issue of concern is that there are many different interpretations of history. Of particular relevance to our theme, there has developed an orthodox view of history which goes something like this: humans used to be primitive and uncivilised and the modern world represents the apex & culmination of civilisation. This view is arguably wrong on two counts. Firstly, any analysis of history demonstrates that we are constantly changing and evolving in intellectual, social & technological ways. In the history of this planet, human beings have been around for a mere fraction of time and there is absolutely no reason to suggest that we've somehow "made it" now and no further radical change is necessary or possible. Secondly, there is some apparent archaeological & geological evidence that advanced societies, more technologically developed than ours, did exist in the distant past, perhaps wiped out by a global flood. Many legends worldwide refer to this, also indicating that they collapsed due to some sort of inherent "wickedness". Fascinating & controversial though this might be, it is not part of the theme of this book. For those interested in such theories, the ideas presented here will not be contradictory to them and can sit comfortably alongside them. It should be noted that the timelines mentioned in this chapter are amenable to challenge and experts do indeed differ. They are approximate, designed to show a generalised pattern of development and while efforts have been made to be accurate, they may be contradicted by other sources.

Transition 1. Use of Fire.

There is a continuous line of development between the first use of fire and todays thermonuclear weapons. The more they are discussed, and their use considered, the more likely the possibility is that humans, in their present form, will cease to exist at all. That present form, anatomically modern humans, dates from approximately 250,000 years ago. From this date, the first indisputable remains of the firepit are evident. While the use of primitive tools derives from an earlier date, both these and the use of fire constitute the first appearance of what we call "technology" and the first incidence of the burning of wood; carbon dioxide producing materials. The use of ever more sophisticated and widespread technologies is one issue that separates out humans from the innumerable other animal species on the planet. This first technological development had profound ramifications for the ability of humans to survive. Firstly, it meant that we could survive in colder climates. While the first *homo sapiens* developed in Eastern Africa, the evidence of fire was in Europe and the Middle East, indicating a northward migration.

Fire would also have been an important factor in keeping

wild carnivore animals at bay, thus helping the human population to increase. The development of the firepit also led to the barbecue and the potential for increasing the range & digestibility of different foodstuffs. Not only did the pleasure of eating increase, but also the increasing availability of nutrients probably contributed to the refinement of the human form; particularly an increase in the relative size of the brain. The brain is a very energy consuming organ; energy derived from more sophisticated foodstuffs. Relative brain size also indicates increasing mental abilities, suggesting that the first use of fire became, over time, a self-perpetuating means of enhancing further technological prowess and other social developments. Also, fire has both a creative and destructive use; beneficial and harmful aspects. To discriminate, learn about and communicate these differences was greatly enhanced by the next major transition.

Transition 2. Development of Language

While many species of animals and birds make sounds to communicate between individuals, the descended larynx of the first anatomically modern humans vastly increased the range of sounds that could be made. The development of spoken language was probably a very gradual process of development. However, scholarly interpretation tends to favour a date of about 40,000 years ago for the use of language similar to our modern use. This includes a shared understanding of what different words mean and the use of syntax; the complex arrangement of different words and phrases to convey detailed meaning. A similar date is also held for the first more widespread appearance of art. Language and Art both can both be said to represent the appearance of "culture"; information, ideas and meanings that can be communicated, using symbols, within a group of people who share an understanding of what those words and symbols mean.

Combined with the increase in brain size occurring within our first transition, the development of language also instigated an enhanced development of abstract and conceptual thinking. Because words are usually associated with tangible things, objects and events, a specific type of mental development became possible. Language is both a representative system, where specific words represent specific things ("That is a fire and it's hot") and also a conceptual system ("I'm feeling cold… I'll light a fire"). The fire in this example doesn't exist now, rather its conceived to exist in the future.; an abstract concept. Thus, language opened up the possibility of two distinct types of cognition which have persisted to this day, and which still preoccupy us to different degrees. Firstly an orientation within time and space; the ability to plan for the future and reflect on the past ("fire warmed me in the past and it will do so again"). Generally speaking, this orientation is based on the pursuit of pleasure and the avoidance of pain. Secondly, the ability to relate external events to a separate something called "me"; the development of self-awareness. In the modern day, the socialisation of young children follows a similar pattern. Usually, the first word attached to a new-born is their name. Subsequent development of language concerns the naming of other humans, objects & events within their environment and their manipulation. This in turn sets a basic human orientation; the seeking of pleasure and the avoidance of pain for "me". It can be seen that the transitions discussed in this chapter are not merely things that happened a long time ago, but foundational developments that influence how we are today and that frame our responses to the experiences and situations we encounter.

Language and the ability to communicate ideas and concepts between people also rapidly advanced the development of the social order. Sewing and sewn garments appeared, as did the first musical instruments around this same date of 40,000 years ago approximately. Tool-making became more widespread and sophisticated. Hunting techniques developed as did probably co-operation to be more successful in the hunt. Language enabled information about the world to be communicated more widely, which plants were beneficial and in what way, what tools could be used for what purposes, etc.. The development of language was a definite game changer.

Transition 3. The Agricultural Revolution

The transitions touched on so far led people to develop small social communities possessing the ability to use & develop simple technologies and interpersonal communications. It's reasonable to assume that the life of the community revolved around keeping warm, comfortable, socialising, breeding, probably a fair bit of gossip and squabbling... and eating. The means of finding food was hunting animals for meat and the gathering of plants; the hunter-gatherer life. This lifestyle is still evident in remote communities in the present day, although rapidly dying out due to encroachment of the modern world.

The evidence for the first appearance of agriculture was about 10,500– 11,500 years ago in the Fertile Crescent region of the Middle East; the modern-day countries of Iraq, Turkey, Syria, Lebanon, Israel, Palestine and Egypt. It probably involved the cultivation of selected species of wild grasses and other edible plants, fruits and husbandry of animals. No longer did people need to go out looking for food. Instead the food supply was brought to the people. This meant that communities could develop in specific fixed locations. There were several enduring consequences for the life of the community. It meant that a given area of land could be more productive of food, which in turn led to increased population growth. That population could also develop socially, having more time for leisure, reflection and pursuits other than those required for simple survival. It also meant that the status of women changed. Hitherto women had a specific role within the community as gatherers of plants. The development of agriculture led to a loss of status and a progressive subjugation of women over the next 12,000 years or so, before it began to radically and consciously change in the 20th century.

Because more food could be produced and a larger community supported, more specialist social roles could be created to sustain a more stable & growing population, living in a more permanent physical location. House building started. Within the hunter-gatherer system, everyone was involved in the same basic life task. It was an egalitarian society. However, the agricultural system engendered a more sedentary way of living with greater options for varied lifestyles. This in turn led to social inequalities as people began to differ in terms of power, wealth & status. Where those differences existed, competition & jealousies between people also began to develop, both within the community and also with other communities. The stage was being set for a further transition where those dynamics could be effectively managed and integrated into a collective lifestyle.

The development of agriculture also fostered changes in the way that people co-existed with the environment. For the hunter-gatherers, the environment was a source of "gifts", food & medicines, and there is evidence that that gift was respected and honoured through rituals, community festivals and special measures at specific places. In the modern world, indigenous societies retain that consciousness of respect for the environment; the mother earth who supports her children. However, the agricultural revolution spawned a new more utilitarian attitude to the environment. It changed over time from being a gift to being a resource. It marks the beginning of the modification and destruction of natural ecosystems and the first seeds of a belief that nature exists solely for our use & exploitation.

The agricultural community, focussed around the production of food and other trades & crafts to facilitate this, was the dominant societal model for much of the world up until the birth of the 18th century industrial revolution and the onset of modernity. In Britain, most people lived in village communities until this transition.

Transition 4. Civilisation: States & Empires

"Civilisation" is a challenging term to define, but in the

context of the chapter it is referred to as the appearance of cities & the social, technological & organisational systems to support them; large structured communities of people. The first recorded appearance of the city was about 7000 years ago in the area of modern-day Turkey. Çatalhöyük was believed to be home to about ten thousand people. However, most history books refer to the Sumerian civilisation as the first true civilisation as we currently understand the term. This is usually dated to about 3500 BCE in Mesopotamia; modern day Iraq. The broad outlines of life at this time are strikingly similar to the modern world in many important ways. It can be difficult to comprehend just how radical the transition was, in terms of the sheer number, scope and scale of innovations that occurred at this time, and which set the pattern for millennia to come.

To build the cities required firstly a sophisticated ability for monumental masonry; the working of stone. This in turn required much more specialised tools and building techniques. While in times past, muscle power was the main source of energy, the Sumerians had mechanical devices to aid & supplement human efforts. Initially this involved the use of animals, such as oxen, but later they harnessed the power of wind and water. They also had a more sophisticated engineering technology; wheels, levers, pulleys and gears. Not only were they able to work stone, but also were able to construct edifices that would challenge us nowadays to reproduce with the same level of accuracy and sophistication. This had led some scholars to propose that they were in possession of technologies that have become lost to the modern world, or even the subjects of extra-terrestrial visitation.

The Sumerians also had writing, which had enormous implications. It meant that written records were preserved and which today can help us understand the life of that time. Of special note amongst these, is the "Epic of Gilgamesh", which amongst other things communicates the details of a prior civilisation that had been destroyed in a great flood; possibly the source of much of the innovations of this historical era. It is somewhat of a mystery as to how so many of the features of this civilisation seemed to suddenly appear out of nowhere.

Writing also had enormous benefits in maintaining the social and political structures of the society, which were of a magnitude apparently dwarfing what came before. That society had a centralised hierarchical structure, at the head of which was the ruler; the king. Below the central authority was a stratified & highly organised class system, held in place by laws (with the means of enforcing them) and what we now term "religion" as governing principles keeping the people in their place. The King and his court, together with the priesthood, occupied the highest class levels, enjoying sophisticated clothing, arts, leisure and ornaments. Slaves, another

Sumerian innovation, were at the bottom of the pile. Women, although able to own property and able to occupy certain positions in society, were expected to become wives, looking after the household & children (when not at school) while the men could get on with more important stuff! All this meant, for possibly the first time in human history, many people could now live not from their own labour but from the labour of others; enjoying a greater level of affluence than those who provided it. With greater material riches also came a belief that it indicated a superiority of character and sense of entitlement.

The maintenance of the king's authority was preserved by an army of professional soldiers, with weaponry. The army also had a role to expand, by violence & warfare, the geographical area of the civilisation, such that it became an empire. The effectiveness of the army was reinforced by the use of metals in the weaponry. While the use of metals, copper, had begun in an earlier era, it was at this time that metal working developed to include, for instance, smelting and the use of bronze; an amalgam of copper.

Agriculture, also became more developed, chiefly through the use of the plough and irrigation. In addition, this time saw the development of growing specific cereals, wheat & barley, rather than simply wild grasses, as in earlier times. Agriculture became a much more labour intensive & productive process to support the growing population. The chief city of the early Sumerian period, Uruk, was believed to support a central population of around 40,000 with 80,000 – 90,000 living nearby; the suburbs.

The Sumerians were also the first people to delineate and measure the passing of time. They had a calendar that defined months as a period of 30 days. Each day was divided into 12 periods of time, which were in turn divided into 30 smaller periods. It's easy to see how these figures later developed into the 24 hour day, each hour divided into 60 minutes; each minute comprising 60 seconds.

This has been a very brief and rudimentary introduction to the fourth of the transitions. Much more detailed information is widely available for what is a fascinating historical period. However, it has hopefully shown how the basic details of our current type of society & way of life have a long precedent. The basic pattern established by the Sumerians was more or less reproduced, with variations & historical interludes, by ensuing civilisations up to the present day. The great civilisation of Egypt came slightly later from about 3200 BCE and gave to the world Mathematics & Medicine. Further great civilisations included Crete & Greece (from 3000 BCE), India (from 2400 BCE), China (from 1500 BCE), Africa (from 1000 BCE), Rome (from 625 BCE), Persia (from 550 BCE) and the Mayans & Aztecs of central America between 300-1540 CE. It should be noted that all these great civilisations rose, flourished, declined and then died in that form. There is no reason to think that our current civilisation is any different.

Transition 5. European Colonisation of the World

All the major civilisations have been both victims and perpetrators of colonialism; the process of expansion of the geographical area of the root civilisation by violent conquest of others. However, the period of European colonisation was of a much greater magnitude, impact & longevity. The imposition of European culture has had a far-reaching influence over just about every nation on earth. Despite occupying only 8% of the planetary land mass, the period between 1492 and 1914 AD saw European powers colonise a massive 84% of the world. The largest empire in world history, the British Empire, at its height controlled the lives of 412 million people; almost a quarter of the global population.

By the 14th century, medieval European civilisation was coming to its end, leading to the intellectual and economic revival that we now call The Renaissance. The Roman Catholic Church was the dominant religion throughout western Europe, with a strong missionary impulse to convert others to this faith. Islam was the dominant faith throughout large areas of the Middle East, Asia and north Africa; spawning a culture of great sophistication & learning. There were extensive trading & mutual learning links between these cultural groups and also further afield to India, China and Japan; all distinct and unique cultures living more or less independently of each other.

The beginning of the era of European colonisation is mostly closely associated with the name of Christopher Columbus; a self-educated Italian mariner born in 1451 in the republic of Genoa. At this time, the European powers wanted to find sea, rather than land, routes to the far east, where there was much money to be made through trade. The earlier Greek civilisation had by the 3rd century BCE deduced that the Earth was a spherical ball. Armed with this knowledge, Columbus set sail in 1492 heading west, convinced that this would lead him to the promised source of silk, spices and riches that lay to the east of Europe.

As we now know, it wasn't the far east he arrived at, but rather the "new world". Landing in the Bahamas, he also visited Cuba before claiming Haiti on behalf of his employer, Spain: "Nice place... it's ours now.". Installed as governor, one of his first acts was to capture some of the local residents and take them back to Spain, presumably against their will. Columbus's rule was characterised by brutality & violence before he was removed from post, the rest of his life dedicated to protracted legal challenges against his government for what he believed was owed to him. To cruelty, enslavement and sour grapes could also be added ignorance: he never renounced the belief that his voyages had actually taken him to the far east.

Columbus established the template for what then came after as the new emerging nation states of Holland, France, Britain, Portugal and Spain embarked upon an orgy of world conquest and money making; imposing inherited European systems of law, governance, religion and education wherever they went. To accomplish this, they were aided by superior weaponry, principally guns and steel swords, against which their victims could not compete. Central to their motivation was a belief that European culture and people were superior to the "primitive & uncivilised" peoples they conquered, thus justifying the dehumanisation of others and establishing the enduring & dangerous myth of white supremacy, which haunts us to this day.

It's worth pointing out that while many pre-conquest cultures became weakened or disappeared, the psychological & emotional influence of colonialism on the conquered peoples has not gone away. The economies of European nation states benefitted tremendously from the resources & riches that they grabbed, a fact never forgotten by the many countries who were exploited, underpinning many of the geopolitical tensions in the world today. Chief among these is the consequences of the extensive transatlantic slave trade. While slavery had been widely practised both in Africa itself and the ancient Mediterranean world, it had practically died out in medieval Europe. However, in 1502, well into the colonial period, the decimation of the local population by the colonists created a labour shortage for the new European enterprises. The suggested remedy was to import black people to do the work, and thus the great abomination of slavery commenced. Britain's involvement in this began with the figure of John Hawkins, who in 1562 captured slaves from West Africa, before transporting and selling his "cargo" in the West Indies. This trade continued until formally abolished in Britain in 1833, directly touching the lives of some 3.1 million unfortunate souls, plus many more friends, relatives & descendants. That's just Britain's contribution. The fact of African slavery, the major contributor to the presence of black people in the United States and the West Indies, before emigration to Britain, has resulted in a "wound" within the psyche of black people of African origin, not to mention the scourge of racism. This is a global issue that continues to be unresolved.

Transition 6. The 18th Century Industrial Revolution.

The last major historical transition, the Industrial Revolution, with swift beginnings and a gradual development into modernity, began a process of building on the perceived benefits of previous transitions; especially the global trade brought by the period of European colonisation. It carried a heightened emphasis on technology, economic & political development and radical changes to the majority human lifestyle. The subject is dealt with in detail in the next Chapter, showing both the speed at which it initially occurred (of relevance to the changes that are needed now) and also the specific technological, legal and structural issues that kick-started it. Most importantly it puts it in the context of an intellectual revolution that also took place around the same time and which we now term "the Enlightenment". Throughout Europe, the freedom from toil & the ensuing affluence that European conquests enabled for some, initiated the growth of an intellectual elite of thinkers and writers, mainly men, who laid down the theoretical principles that have guided us into the modern world. These principles, ideas or "story" both define what mainstream thinking regards as normal, and also come into conflict with the new ideas that began to develop in the 20th century to supersede them.

Transition 7. Global Transition into Sustainability

All the previous transitions mentioned have occurred because in some way they initiated a leap forward in the perceived self-interests of the human population. At every stage of the process, each transition has disregarded and diminished slightly, with increasing impact, the viability of the natural world, the environment and the well-being of some people. For most of these transitions, up until the industrial revolution, it's not really been regarded as an issue. Nature has continued to thrive, despite occasional extinctions, usually due to over-exploitation. The effect on humans however has been dual. On the one hand, the increasing affluence of the majority has been regarded as an overall benefit, justifying the suffering inflicted on others. However, that has now changed. Due to a combination of population size, unrestrained economic development, environmental destruction, enhanced weaponry combined with the growth of a sensitive goodwill towards others and most importantly scientific research & understanding of our impact on the natural world and each other, the perceived benefits of earlier transitions have brought us to a critical point. We are catastrophically destroying the natural systems of air, water, soil and climate on which we depend for our very existence, at an accelerating rate, as well as human happiness. This is not sustainable, which is why the current period of change is regarded as a transition into sustainability. The transitions of the past suggest to some that this can be rectified by the development of new technologies. It worked in the past. However, one cutting-edge technology of the moment, so-called "artificial intelligence" points to the complete opposite; the displacement of human culture, jobs, art & language. The intellectual backlash, concerns and fears over this are growing. However, there is by no means a universal consensus that that is the case. In fact, growing in parallel with the deepening crisis in which we are immersed, there is also a growing atmosphere of conflict & division regarding the assumed facts of the whole system crisis in all its aspects. It's no exaggeration to suggest that it is a kind of "world war"; not just the numerous violent conflicts brought to our awareness every day, through the media or direct experience, but also a war of ideas, opinions and attitudes. We can't go back to the past, we can't carry on as we are now and there is no agreed path into the future.

Following on from Chapter 2 about the Industrial Revolution & the Enlightenment, Chapter 3 looks at specific elements of our current economic system that derive from this, the current impacts on societal stability and how more recent historical developments open up the possibility of a radical change of approach. Chapter 4 similarly looks at our structure of politics and governance; its origins and the suggested changes that are beginning to emerge. In Chapter 5, the whole principle of science and its by-product, technology, is examined, pointing to the way that recent discoveries challenge the very foundations of our prior understanding of the universe and our place within it. Chapter 6 summarises the way that a 20th century enlightenment, an outpouring of new thinking, undermines both the assumptions of the past and also provides a coherent framework for the future that is happening now; albeit in conflict with much of mainstream thinking and vested interest groups. Chapter 7 puts all these issues into the context of a human evolutionary development; an evolution not of our physical form but rather of human consciousness & the resultant society... the being of our human being-ness. It can be conceived as a "coming of age" and emergence into adulthood following the long childhood & painful growth into maturity of earlier times.

Chapter 2

The Industrial Revolution

The previous chapter mapped out a progressive series of transitions, or significant steps, in the ongoing process of human social development. Each of those steps introduced new principles & practices that humans adopted and which have become integrated into our current society, lifestyles, ways of thinking and behaviours. In all ways, one thing has led to another. The innovations of one period naturally led to the next, initiating a new phase of development. Prior to the Industrial Revolution, the period of European Colonisation had established a society where we Europeans believed that we were entitled to rule the world, and we did. A network of international trade had been established, which had created a deep & enduring social division. On the one hand, the masses of people still lived lives of toil, most usually based around agriculture & artisan crafts in village communities, while an emergent middle and upper class had a more affluent lifestyle; often city based and enriched by the financial opportunities that colonisation had created.

Pre-revolutionary rural life for the masses in 17th and

18th century Europe was characterised by poverty, poor food and hygiene, social isolation and lack of formal education. Fewer than 1 in 5000 were literate and old age was considered to start at 35. The majority of the population lived in small village communities. Everyone knew everyone else and the needs of the community itself was the organising principle of society. The community was more or less self-sufficient, in terms of food, clothing, housing, entertainment, relationships, religion, child rearing. What we now call social mobility was practically non-existent.

The Industrial Revolution changed all that, again in a series of stages over 200 years or so. The orthodox view is that the actual revolution has encompassed at least 4 mini-transitions and is still ongoing, with the last one covering the period from 1950 to 1990, and a new one beginning to take place now. Each stage has marked a period of new economic development, use of new technologies, new employment patterns, new educational priorities and radical changes in majority lifestyle. Each step has also created a widening division between rich and poor, a progressive erosion of individual quality of life, an accelerating destruction of nature and a new set of problems. Let's look at each stage one by one.

The first stage took place from the mid-1700s, with an especially significant two-year period around 1733. The first innovation, a technological one, was the invention of the Flying Shuttle in 1733. Up to this point, weaving was a cottage industry, carried out in the villages and usually home-based. With the invention of the flying shuttle, it made possible industrial-scale weaving, carried out in a factory. The potential of the invention was that the output, the amount of woven goods, could be 8 times greater in the same amount of time. Entrepreneurs and those who already possessed wealth glimpsed an opportunity to increase that wealth. However, something else was needed to bring the vision to fruition and that was a legal issue.

Thomas Newcomen (1664-1729), an ironmonger by trade & Baptist lay preacher, had in 1712 invented the "atmospheric engine"; in effect the world's first steam engine. It had a very practical use. Mines for coal, and in Newcomen's case tin, were severely limited in the amount of product that could be extracted & monetised, and hence not that attractive as investment opportunities. The problem was that if you dig a hole in the ground, it rapidly fills up with water. Newcomen's invention, and its application as a pump to draw water out of tin mines, suddenly made mining a more viable economic proposition because mines could now go much deeper. However, being an inventor and eager to try and make money out of his invention, he patented the device and hence made it not widely available for use. By a serendipitous twist of fate, the patent expired in 1733;

the same year as the invention of the flying shuttle. This suddenly made possible the large-scale extraction of the coal, iron ore and other metals necessary to feed the rapidly approaching industrial age. The soon-to-be large scale burning of coal marked the beginning of the build-up of atmospheric carbon dioxide; the key driver of climate change.

However, this was yet to come. The first mills were water-powered, thanks to Richard Arkwright (1732-1792). Born in my hometown of Preston, Lancashire, Arkwright took the earlier invention of the flying shuttle, and other devices, to build the first fully functioning mechanised factory in 1771. A wondrous structure it was too. By necessity built adjacent to a river, water was first diverted through a network of channels, to drive a large water wheel; the primary source of power. Through a complex network of gears placed throughout the factory, this in turn drove multiple machines placed over the several floors of the mill. For the initial 200 workers, mainly women and children as young as 7, the noise must have been horrendous. The 6 weekly shifts ran from 6am to 6pm. Any worker, young or old, unable to get through the entire shift, for whatever reason, was fined not merely that days wages but also another extra day as well. For perhaps the first time, and certainly not the last, the "needs of the economy" and humanitarian social conscience came into conflict. Arkwright, or his managers, later raised the minimum age of workers from

7 to 10 years of age.

Child labour was not the only negative by-product of the industrial revolution. As water powered factories gradually gave way to coal-fired steam, the whole industry, together with the workers, gradually moved into the cities. The workers in particular, low paid, were forced into inner-city neighbourhoods, in turn driving more affluent residents into the suburbs. By the time of the 1830s, a public health report in Liverpool[3] discovered that nearly a third of the total population of the city were living in cellars; insanitary, overcrowded and miserable. The lack of sanitation & clean water in particular, led to a heightened proliferation of nasty infectious diseases. Poor nutrition was widespread, further exacerbating poor health.

While pre-revolution life in the villages had been hard, life in the cities was even harder. In the villages, the life of the community had been the organising principle of the society. From a life governed by the changing seasons, a new organising principle now emerged; the demands of the workplace. Those demands were harsh.

---

3. The Liverpool Cholera Epidemic of 1832 and Anatomical Dissection — Medical Mistrust and Civil Unrest, SEAN BURRELL and GEOFFREY GILL. Journal of the History of Medicine and Allied Sciences, Vol. 60, No. 4 (OCTOBER 2005), pp. 478-498 (21 pages). Published By: Oxford University Press

When once the day began with the rising sun, it now began when the factory whistle blew. When once the individual was autonomous and their own master, often with time for a quick chat with friends, a rest or a diversion, now the worker was enslaved by repetitive boring tasks, always to be carried out quicker and more efficiently than yesterday. The age of time & motion studies had begun. By the end of the long day, the attractions of the local pub must have seemed welcome, and indeed they did. The link between unsatisfying work and alcoholism has a long pedigree and continues to this day.

Socially, the expectation was that the man of the family was the provider. Such an assumption was music to the ears of the factory owners, who soon realised that it gave them justification for paying women up to half what they paid men for doing the same tasks. They also believed that women were better suited than men for doing soul-destroying repetitive work. Quite why they might think this is not clear. However, it did set a precedent for a behaviour on the part of some employers that continues to this day.

The burning of vast amounts of coal led to serious environmental hazards. Not only was the air in the cities visibly polluted, driving the incidence of a vast array of respiratory illnesses, but it also marked an acceleration of the build-up of greenhouse gases in the atmosphere, again driving the climate change that we are challenged with today. Not only the factories were to blame for this, as the growing use of coal powered steam engines naturally led to the initial development & rapid expansion of the railway system. However, some of the worst excesses of the time were partially mitigated by what we now regard as the second phase of the industrial revolution; the use of gas, electricity and oil for power. In Britain, the widespread use of gas for heating & lighting began around 1812 when Frederick Winsor launched a company to build a public gas works. The gas produced was distributed to customers through a network of underground pipes. Much cleaner than coal, the enterprise was a success and widely supported for a number of reasons; ease of use, reliability & efficiency. Now the most widely used fuel for domestic heating, the burning of gas again greatly magnified the build-up of atmospheric carbon dioxide.

The early 19th century was a time of tremendous economic and social change. Much of this was due to the work of Michael Faraday, who in 1821 discovered that if you move a magnet through a coil of wire, it produces an electric current. This led him to invent the electric motor; the same device that powers your washing machine, lawnmower and a multiplicity of electric devices throughout your home and the wider society. It took a few years, until 1870 in fact, for Thomas Edison to build the first electrical generator, followed by the first public electricity supply in 1881 to power all this. Mind you, the discovery of electricity has a much earlier tradition, being attributed to the ancient Greeks. A man named Thales discovered that if you rub a piece of amber with silk, it attracts lightweight objects like feathers; static electricity. The Greek word for amber is "eelectron", which where the name comes from.

While gas and electricity were used domestically, industry was still dominated by coal as a source of power. The prevalence of coal led a Scottish chemist, James Young, in 1847 to carry out research at the Riddings coal mine in Debyshire; the source of much coal for the factories in that area. On one of his expeditions there, he noticed a thick liquid seeping out from one of the coal seams. On further investigation back at the lab, he found that he was able to refine it into two usable products; a light liquid that could be burnt in lamps and a thicker liquid that was an effective lubricant. The age of oil had begun; which was destined to become one of the principal drivers of the global economy. Especially one of its by-products, plastic, has become so deeply integrated & embedded into our collective lifestyle that it's difficult to imagine life without it, even though the dangers from plastics pollution are becoming ever more apparent.

Oil to petrol to cars. The first known example of a car dates to 1672 in China. It was steam driven, and steam remained the primary energy source for much of the car's early development. It couldn't actually carry passengers, being more of a novelty than a practical transport proposition. That privilege goes to the device created by Nicolas-Joseph Cugnot in 1769, again steam driven. The arrival of the internal combustion engine dates to the early 1800s, with the first commercially available petrol driven car attributed to Carl Benz in 1886. However, the first popularly available car was built by the US Ford Motor Company in 1908. Much of its ensuing success was down to the innovations of its creator, Henry Ford (1863-1947).

While the first cars were produced in specialist workshops, Ford was influenced in his business methods by other sources. On a visit to a slaughterhouse in Chicago, he studied the way that pigs were slaughtered and butchered. He observed that the animals were hung from hooks on a moving conveyor belt, which then travelled through the building. On their journey from the open field to the bacon butty, different people performed different tasks at each stage of the process. It gave him a great idea. The same principle could be applied to the manufacture of motor cars. He could now build cars much faster, more efficiently and with greater profits. Workers could be paid more and the era of "mass production" in larger factories commenced. The main disadvantage was that workplace satisfaction & sense of meaning, the essential human pride in doing a good job, became much more diminished. It could be said that the advent of "Fordism" also marks the tangible beginning of a profound shift in the way that human beings are related to economic activity. 1920, the year when the Model T Ford reached its apex of production as the car of the people, was also the year that human beings were first redefined as "consumers"; a somewhat derogatory term, now in universal use.

The year 1967 arguably marks the beginning of the third phase of the industrial revolution, an era that introduced a technology integral to almost every aspect of most people's lives today. In that year US company Hewlett-Packard introduced a new term into common use: personal computer. The first computer was actually created over 2000 years ago, again in ancient Greece. The Antikythera mechanism was used to predict astronomical positions and eclipses. A purely mechanical device, it bore little resemblance to the proliferation of laptops, tablets and smartphones in use today. For that, we are initially indebted to Alan Turing who invented computer science in 1936. His original machine was created to solve an important mathematical & philosophical problem; how do we decide what is true or false[4].

---

4. The problem that Turing attempted to solve is known as the Entscheidungsproblem. Briefly stated, it asks if in any formal language we make a logical statement in that language, is there a procedure that will evaluate the truth value of that statement and output an answer; "true" or "false"?

The procedure he worked out is what we now call an "algorithm"; used today to determine what products for sale and what information, irrespective of whether it's true or not, pops up on our device screen.

Throughout the 1970s and beyond, computers began to dominate the workplace and heralded the age of automation. Taking place within a sequence of events since the 1700s that has seen human creativity, satisfaction & meaning become progressively secondary to the demands of economic growth, computerisation removed it almost completely, except for hands punching away at keyboards. When computers were first introduced, the vision presented to us was that they would eliminate drudgery. They may well have eliminated some, but instead introduced a new form. Nowadays, almost every profession or job involves, to a greater or lesser degree, sitting in front of a keyboard & screen, while computers have been afforded an almost mythical status as "truth-tellers". If what a person states to be true is contradicted by what the computer says, then the computer version is assumed to be correct; resulting in an escalating frequency of injustices. The drudgery of many repetitive industrial processes has been replaced by a new burden of endless emails, spam, backache and new forms of computer cybercrime.

This latter has not strictly speaking derived from computers as such, rather the fourth phase of the industrial revolution as it has come to dominate our lives; the internet. The origins of the net began with the Cold War of the 1950s. At the time, the global superpowers of the USA and the Soviet Union were both in possession of thermonuclear weapons. There was a tremendous and widespread fear of an unexpected & deadly attack. In response to this, American military intelligence realised that, in the event of a nuclear attack, it would need some sort of communication system that could survive the attack. At that time, early computers were in use, although very different from today. The computing power of today's average pocket-sized smartphone would then have required at least a whole roomful, if not more, of floor to ceiling equipment. The technology was mainly confined to the military establishment and universities. The first soviet-proof communication system linked together four university computers, in separate locations, into a network; the first inter-net. The thinking was that if one computer was knocked out, the other three would retain the integrity of the system.

Some computer systems still employ a similar system, but for most people their experience of the internet is as the World Wide Web. All website addresses that begin with www are part of this. The idea was first suggested by a Briton; Tim Berners-Lee in 1989. A computer scientist by profession, his interest had developed during a childhood spent learning about the electronics of his model train set. His initial idea was based around the creation of a webserver, a computer-based web browser, a computer language, html, and the use of phone lines to transmit information. His boss at the time expressed an astonishing lack of prescience by his response to Tim's idea: "vague". Undeterred, Tim ploughed on. Years later, a 25 strong panel of world leaders & academics[5] came up with a list of the 80 most important inventions and developments that have contributed to the modern world. The world wide web came in at number one, the panel describing it as: *"The fastest growing communications medium of all time, the Internet has changed the shape of modern life forever. We can connect with each other instantly, all over the world."*

Tim Berners-Lee launched his invention with a large degree of idealism. He originally envisaged it as a communication medium for the free exchange of information & knowledge, with the emphasis on "free". Indeed, the early years of the web were this, a function which continues to this day. However, it wasn't long before the drivers of economic growth monetised it as a vehicle for shopping, turning it into the major cause of the decline of town centres as shopping, recreational, cultural and social centres. In many ways, the internet has displaced human-to-human interaction. Town

---

5. Source: Innovation Management. < https://innovationmanagement.se/2018/02/01/imagine-a-bigger-better-world-an-innovative-leap-by-sir-tim-berners-lee/>

centres are now more often places where people wander around staring at their phone, unconscious of what is taking place around them. Computers in all their forms, plus the software that runs on them, have become not just another product to buy and sell, but rather now dictate how we live, what our attitudes are, what we value and what we should do about it.

It's almost as if humans are becoming superfluous to the world that the industrial revolution has created. In fact, that is the exact point of what some regard as the fifth and final phase of the industrial revolution. Artificial Intelligence, the latest development in computer science, is being heralded as the next big thing; machines that are more intelligent than we are. Despite the protestations of many "intelligent" people that they might well signify the end of human life on this planet, the profits to be made from it are potentially staggering. As the entire history of the industrial revolution has been one of finding ever more inventive ways to make money arguably at the expense of human & planetary well-being, the logic of declaring its many anticipated benefits is obvious. One might well ask, how on earth have we arrived at this point?

The Enlightenment

The Industrial Revolution began in Britain and was adopted worldwide as an economic and social model.

Despite the many uncomfortable situations that it has engendered, all based around financial issues conflicting with humanitarian & environmental concerns, it has also massively improved the standard of living of many, if not most. Compared to what came before, good quality housing, nutrition, healthcare, leisure, education & opportunities for social mobility are now widely available. There is no suggestion that these are equally enjoyed by everyone, but they are what the majority in the developed nations regard as normal, desirable and expected.

However, the industrial revolution didn't happen in a vacuum. The many practical elements of it were only seized upon and put into widespread practice because the minds of educated & powerful people were ready to receive them. We tend to look on the transition of the industrial revolution in terms of technology, lifestyle and economic patterns, just as we frame our current possible responses to the environmental crisis in similar terms. However, underpinning the physical, structural and social changes that happened, there was also taking place an intellectual and philosophical revolution that introduced new ideas and ways of thinking into the collective consciousness; a movement we now call "the enlightenment", spanning the 17th and 18th centuries. Meeting in salons, coffee houses and masonic lodges, groups of educated, mainly men, gathered to lay the intellectual and philosophical foundations of both the

Industrial Revolution and the following centuries, up the modern day. While covering a vast range of scientific, political, moral and economic thinking, their ideas all focussed around the notion that everything in the universe could be rationally explained, classified, measured and manipulated by human intervention. These ideas were considered to be true beyond doubt, until the 20th century when a new enlightenment began to take shape. This chapter examines the ideas of just three influential enlightenment thinkers, showing how their ideas still inform & guide the modern world, also indicating how they are now being slowly replaced by a new intellectual awareness; the subject of chapter 6. Their ideas have become so deeply embedded in our collective consciousness that it's often difficult to imagine any other alternative. And yet, if we are to find a way out of the current whole system crisis, that's precisely what we must do.

Sir Isaac Newton (1642 – 1727), scientist & mathematician, is widely regarded as one of the most influential scientists of all time. In popular mythology, he is perhaps best remembered for an incident where he was sitting under an apple tree and an apple fell on his head. Legend has it that this inspired him to develop the theory of gravity, being somewhat curious as to why the apple, or indeed any other object, always fell directly downward, rather than sideways or upwards. This example shows that Newton, like many other great scientists, had a distinct knack for being able to turn his attentive & enquiring mind to things that everyone was aware of but had never really questioned. His other great quality of personality was the ability to become so inwardly focussed in thought that he would lose all awareness of the outside world, often for hours at a time. In childhood his mother wanted him to become a farmer, a profession Newton hated. On one occasion, she asked him to walk a horse several miles to the next village. Isaac dutifully, albeit resentfully, set off leading the horse by a halter, progressively becoming lost in thought. Upon arriving at the village, he was awakened from a deep reverie by the sound of a crowd surrounding him, laughing. There stood Isaac, his arm still upright holding the halter, but with no horse to be seen. It had bolted away miles back.

These qualities confirm Newton as what we now call a "polymath"; someone who achieves excellence in a wide range of different disciplines. To physics, he could add mathematics, theology, astronomy, natural philosophy and somewhat surprisingly, alchemy, to his range of accomplishments. His achievements that have come down to us includes his work on optics, the composition of light. In mechanics he established his three laws of motion; the basic principles of modern physics as taught in all schools and the foundation of the law of universal gravitation. In the field of mathematics, he was the original discoverer of calculus. His book, *Philosophiae*

Naturalis Principia Mathematica (Mathematical Principles of Natural Philosophy), 1687, is widely regarded as one of the most important works in the entire history of modern science.

Undoubtedly a genius, Newton was also a complex character, who had difficulties in entering into relationships with others. Deeply insecure, depressive, paranoid, vengeful, spiteful, vindictive and prone to outbursts of violent temper, he could also be kind, generous and humble. Indeed he wrote: *"I know not how I seem to others, but to myself I am but a small child wandering upon the vast shores of knowledge, every now and then finding a small bright pebble to content myself with while the vast ocean of undiscovered truth lay before me."*

Perhaps the greatest enduring contribution Newton has made to the modern mind has been to basically establish the concept of nature as a giant "machine" with an identifiable, measurable physical mechanism; a fitting prelude to a materialistic machine age. This idea formed the dominant scientific viewpoint until the 20th century, with the advent of Albert Einstein, the Quantum Theorists and the Gaia hypothesis. For Newton, time and space were the fixed constants in which the universe moved and had its being, whereas Einstein demonstrated that they were not actually fixed, rather varying & mutable according to the perspective of any observer. Quantum mechanics developed this idea further, showing that all phenomena are themselves the product of consciousness, while the Gaia hypothesis is that the entire Earth is itself a unified, conscious, self-regulating being. These new ideas provide a firm counterpoint to the prevailing notion that nature exists purely as a resource, a thing or machine, for us to financially exploit; one of the enduring contributions of our next enlightenment thinker.

The guiding principles of our current governance system, representative democracy, were laid down by English philosopher and physician John Locke (1632-1704). The son of a cavalry captain on the parliamentarian side in the English civil war, Locke was just 16 and at school on the day of the execution of King Charles 1st. The school was just half a mile away from the execution site, but the pupils were forbidden from going to watch it. However, the incident had a deep influence on the course of Locke's life. The King had been found guilty of "a wicked design to erect and uphold in himself an unlimited and tyrannical power to rule according to his will, and to overthrow the rights and liberties of the people."[6] These themes formed the basis of Locke's life work.

A prolific scholar, writer and well connected with the leading figures of his day, Locke is best known as the

---

6. Source: The Royal Family, Historic Royal Speeches and Writings, Charles 1st, < https://www.royal.uk/sites/default/files/media/charlesi.pdf>

founder of political liberalism, a direction arising from his strongly held religious beliefs. Central to his conception of the role of government was a belief that it should exist solely to protect the life and property of its citizens. Such a life, he argued, includes the right to freedom of conscience and religion. He believed that all people are created free and equal, a view reflected 300 years later in the very first line of the 1948 United Nations Declaration of Universal Human Rights: "All human beings are born free and equal in dignity and rights. They are endowed with reason and conscience and should act towards one another in a spirit of brotherhood."

Locke's main political ideas are summarised in the *Two Treatises*, published in 1689. The first treatise is a refutation of the idea of government by a monarchy; a supreme ruler, divinely ordained & hereditary. In this he was hinting that the only type of government that could endure was one based on free public consent. The second treatise goes on to outline his vision of civil government. It begins with a definition of what he calls the "state of nature"; a state of perfect freedom for people to act as they see fit, without needing the permission of others, in accordance with the laws of nature. However, to avoid the state of war that could occur in the natural state, and to protect property, a civil or political society is required. Property is acquired by the act of taking it from nature. The protection of property is thus the main purpose of the civil society. Locke proposed the ideal form of government to be based on a social contract, whereby some of the rights and freedoms of the natural state are surrendered to a representative body, chosen by the majority, enacting laws, and with the option to change that body if it fails in its primary purpose. He declared that revolt against the government was a fundamental right of the people.

John Locke was primarily a philosopher and his conclusions were arrived at after a long & arduous process of intellectual exploration. It is said that his thinking was very closely aligned with that of Sir Isaac Newton. His ideas were incorporated into the United States Constitution and the UK parliamentary system. Indeed, his precepts have become so embedded into our political system as to be now considered self-evident and unquestionable. However, as we shall explore in Chapter 4 on the theme of Politics & Governance, it can be argued that Locke's vision of the civil society is currently crumbling under the weight of its own contradictions.

The notion of the civil society as a necessary institution to protect property, was also one of the core tenets of our third enlightenment thinker, Adam Smith (1723-1790). His major work, *The Wealth of Nations (1776)* is the principle work that established economics as a comprehensive system and subject of academic study as it is today. Known as the "father of free-market capitalism" and the guiding light of the rapid expansion of the industrial economy, he is so highly regarded by some that Alan Greenspan, chairman of the US Federal Reserve from 1987 to 2006, described the Wealth of Nations as "one of the greatest achievements of human intellectual history".[7]

The core of Smith's beliefs is that self-interest and competition, based on human desire for money, success & status, leads to economic prosperity & happiness. By every individual acting in their own exclusive self-interest, it produces an "invisible hand" that promotes a socially desirable end that no-one had envisaged. Furthermore, that end is actually a lot better for everyone than action specifically designed to improve society; in effect, greed is good. Deeply controversial in his own time and ever since, many of Smith's ideas were also contradictory. A clue to this might be found in his character; described by many who knew him to be extravagantly absent-minded and with the habit of talking to himself. The contradictory and self-defeating results of his work, the world his disciples have created, directly contributing to the current global economic malaise are explored in the next chapter.

---

7. Source: The Federal Reserve Board. Remarks by Chairman Alan Greenspan at the Adam Smith Memorial Lecture, Kirkcaldy, Scotland, February 6, 2005. < https://www.federalreserve.gov/boarddocs/speeches/2005/20050206/default.htm>

Chapter 3

Economics & Finance

"Labour was the first price, the original purchase-money that was paid for all things. It was not by gold or by silver, but by labour, that all wealth of the world was originally purchased... Wherever there is great property there is great inequality."
Adam Smith (1723-1790).

The World Health Organization (WHO) predicts that by 2030 clinical depression will be the second largest cause of the global health burden, currently standing at 280 million prescribed cases worldwide, the majority being women (Source: World Health Organisation, March 2023). In the UK alone, Britain's workplace regulator shows that there were nearly a million cases of work-related stress, depression, or anxiety in 2021/22 (Source: Health & Safety Executive). An estimated 17 million working days were lost during this year. One study found that three in ten employees will have a mental
health problem in any one year, mainly depression, stress and anxiety. Bearing in mind that it's now getting much worse, the BBC, in March 2008, reported the

annual cost to the UK economy of time off work at £100 billion, the same as the cost of running the NHS. This was costing every one of us an average of £1700 annually in tax. The implications of this are profound. You are working to pay for the cost of the harmful effects of going to work! Not changing it, just dealing with it. If you don't particularly enjoy work or paying tax, does that make you feel better? And it's not just adults affected. Children and teenagers are experiencing an "intolerable" mental health crisis, with nearly a quarter of girls now self-harming.

Of course, it could be argued that all this is maintaining the health of the economy, especially the international pharmaceutical industry in both its legal and illegal aspects, providing work for other people and affluence for us all. In fact, the range of work open to us all will be determined largely by the needs of the economy. From an early description of a network of barter and exchange, the industrial revolution saw the establishment of the banking system and the beginning of the development of modern economic practice. Enlightenment thinker John Locke, 1632-1704, was known as the father of liberalism. As well as expounding the principles of representative democracy and majority rule, Locke stated his belief, in his Second Treatise, that nature on its own provides little of value to society, rather that the labour expended on the exploitation of nature in the creation of goods & services gives it its value. In other words, nature is held to have no value to us, other than as a resource to make money out of. In this one single belief underpinning the principles of the Industrial Revolution, and now governing practically the entire global economy, lies one key to understanding just why we are now faced with both the wholesale destruction & abuse of the natural world, as well the erosion of human wellbeing.

From historical origins as a description of human activity, the servant of what we do, "the economy" has now become our master. It teaches us our role within life, it tells us what to believe in order to be happy, it persuades us to buy stuff we don't really need, it lends us the money (at interest) to buy all this, it provides us with increasingly stressful and insecure work to maintain it all, it charges us to soothe our fears at losing it and finally offers a sub-standard service when we can't cope with it any more!

Do you truly love your work? Do you think that such a thing is in fact possible? Or do you take the view that work is just something that has to be done as painlessly as possible, counting off the days remaining towards retirement, and that "real life" is something that takes place outside of work? For too long, and for too many people, the circumstances of work have been primarily a systemically driven need to survive and manage the inbuilt indebtedness that the financial system has imposed on us, rather than one's "vocation". A small number of people benefit financially from this system, many, if not most worldwide, don´t. The necessity of response to the climate and environmental crisis creates a unique opportunity to consciously re-design the way finance and economics work, in order to sustain a collective lifestyle which places human and natural well-being at the centre of the system, it´s primary objective, rather than the periphery; an unwelcome by-product to deal with... or not. To be honest, as the media constantly reminds us, to do what needs to be done to stop trashing the planet & ourselves, is probably impossible to achieve within the current political/economic system. How have we arrived at this point?

> *"Given how much of the evil and ugliness of the present world can be traced to money, can you imagine what the world will be like when money has been transformed?"*
> Charles Eisenstein, Sacred Economics: Money, Gift and Society in the Age of Transition.

The first historical evidence of the "economy", as a system whereby goods and services are exchanged between people, probably derives from ancient Egypt in about 9000 BC. Barter was evident; a key element in what developed into an advanced civilisation. However, the introduction of money had to wait for another eight and a half thousand years. We could clearly manage OK without it! The Lydian Trite, a coin minted around

600BC in Lydia, modern day Turkey, was made of electrum; an alloy of gold and silver called "white gold" in ancient times. Basically, worth about a month's subsistence, it could buy 11 sheep or 10 goats. The coin was marked with an image of a roaring lion; symbolising strength and authority. To the ancient Lydians, the merchants or "People of the Market", those who handled the coins, enjoyed a higher rank in society than ordinary people. They were the financial elite of their time and maintained the peculiar enduring belief that wealth equates to a superiority of character. The Trite was minted during the reign of King Alyattes; father of the legendary King Croesus, known as the richest man in history. However, it didn't do him much good, as his reputation for everything he touched turning to gold, including his own daughter and his food, has come down to us now, unsurprisingly, as indicating somewhat of a curse. To the ancient Greeks, the story of Croesus served as a cautionary tale on hubris; excessive pride towards or defiance of the gods, leading to a miserable conclusion. It was a warning on not tempting the gods' wrath by thinking of oneself, like Croesus did, as the happiest person in the world; a happiness derived from great wealth.

While by the 4th century a number of coins had been minted in various places, they didn't really have any widespread transformative significance until the introduction of the gold Florin in about 1252. Made in the Republic of Florence, now part of modern-day Italy, it was named after the floral emblem of the City and recognised and accepted across large areas of Europe. The idea rapidly caught on. By the 14th century, in less than a hundred years, about 150 European states and coin issuing authorities were making their own Florins. The English Florin was first minted in 1344, during the reign of Edward III, proving the point that a Pan-European economic alignment has a long tradition. The final English Florin was issued in 1970 as a collector's item; the last coin to be withdrawn due to decimalisation.

The introduction of coinage was accepted because the substance out of which they were made, gold, was held to have the highest value. However, in ancient China, around 118 BC during the Han dynasty, an alternative system developed. Promissory notes made of leather guaranteed that, although having no value of their own, they could be exchanged for gold. Merchants tended to like them because they were a lot easier to carry around than lumps of heavy metal. Later, leather was replaced by paper and banknotes progressively replaced gold exchanges over the next several hundred years for large financial transactions. The concept was introduced to Europe shortly after the first florin had been minted. It took nearly 400 hundred years before the first notes appeared in Sweden; 1661. By the beginning of the Industrial Revolution over the next hundred years, the system was firmly in place; banknotes having value because they could, in theory, be exchanged for gold. This equivalence between currency and gold was only finally ended worldwide in 2013; a fact of great significance when it comes to economic transformation.

Between 1689 and 1697, Britain was waging war against a regular enemy; France. The cause was stopping France from wanting to expand its borders into Europe. War is an expensive business and so in 1694 the Bank of England was founded; a private bank whose principle customer was the Government, which needed to borrow money to finance the conflict. Interest payable on the loan was 8%. The King and Queen of the time, William and Mary, were two of the Banks's original stockholders; a nice earner for the royal family. The same William and Mary, in granting its royal charter, explained that the Bank was founded to 'promote the public Good and Benefit of our People'[8]. With a monopoly on English banking, within 12 days the Bank had managed to inject £1.2 million into the national economy to fund the war effort. Work was created, the rich made a tidy pile and the foundations of a modern growth-oriented capitalist economy were laid; new money created by debt. Everyone a winner?

The founding of the Bank of England was arguably the

---

[8]. Source: Bank of England. <https://www.bankofengland.co.uk/about/history>

key element that catalyzed the 18th century Industrial Revolution. Entrepreneurs could now borrow large sums of money to finance the factories, resources and equipment to get it all going. However, the principles on which the new industrial economy would evolve largely came from enlightenment thinker Adam Smith, 1723-1790. Known today as the father of economics and capitalism, Smith laid the foundations of modern free market economic thinking, based on the principle that self-interest and competition lead to economic prosperity. His classic work "The Wealth of Nations" (published 1776) established 3 core ideas guiding mainstream economic thinking to this day. Firstly, that the accumulation of wealth and material goods leads to and produces happiness, leading directly to the modern ingrained belief in fluctuations of Gross Domestic Product (GDP) being a measure of collective well-being. Once basic needs of warmth, shelter and sustenance have been provided, there is little evidence that further wealth alone results in enduring happiness. His second key idea was that the great wealth of just a few people benefits everyone; a viewpoint now widely discredited. Finally, he established the principle that free market capitalism is the best way to end poverty. Nowadays, many people believe the exact opposite.

> *"Civil government... is in reality instituted for the defence of the rich against the poor."*
>
> *Adam Smith*

The UK-based Adam Smith Institute, along with other organisations, seeks to preserve his legacy as a think tank and government adviser on UK economic policy. The current institute president, Madsen Pirie, is on record as describing the activities of the organisation as "we propose things which people regard as being on the edge of lunacy. The next thing you know, they're on the edge of policy".[9] It is best known as a NeoLiberal think tank and lobbying body. What exactly is Neo-Liberalism?

The story begins with the Great Depression of the 1930s. A crazy situation had developed where ordinary Americans had been persuaded to borrow money, at interest, in order to invest in stocks and shares, which would generate for them more money than they had borrowed. The economy was growing so fast that no-one could possibly lose. However, most closely established with events on October 24, 1929, "Black Thursday", the stock market crashed and triggered the great depression. Millions of people suddenly found themselves in unsustainable debt. Between 1929 and 1932, the economic shock affected most countries across the world, some effects lasting until World War II. Neither rich nor poor countries were exempt from the effects; collapsing incomes, trade devastated, mass

---

9. Source: Adam Smith Institute: Rebooting Britain with Dr Madsen Pirie, 20th July, 2016. < https://www.adamsmith.org/events/rebooting-britain-with-dr-madsen-pirie>

unemployment and widespread poverty.

In response to this, economists proposed policies that would try to avoid further economic destabilisation and the social problems that arose from it. The thinking was that 19th century free-market economic practices, established in the Industrial Revolution, had led to the stock market crash and ensuing depression. In practice, this meant that economists worked closely with politicians to devise interventionist policies that would seek to regulate & control economic practices in order to create socially desirable outcomes. The British economist John Maynard Keynes was a key figure in this process and his ideas largely dominated UK political/economic policy until the advents of Margaret Thatcher (UK) in 1979 and Ronald Reagan (US) in 1981.

Keynes was one of the main architects of the 1944 Bretton Woods agreement. Under this system, the value of gold was pegged to the US dollar, which was in turn pegged to the other 44 participating world currencies, including the British pound. The agreement resulted in the creation of two institutions enduring to this day; the International Monetary Fund and the World Bank. These bodies were initially founded to regulate world trade, with a specific brief to stabilise currencies and support nations that had been financially devastated by the second world war. The Bretton Woods agreement collapsed in the early 1970s when US president Richard

Nixon announced that dollars could no longer be exchanged for gold. There wasn't enough of it.

While the general consensus was that the great depression, producing severely decreased economic activity, poverty & unemployment, was a failure of free market economics, not everyone agreed. Amongst others, the Austrian-British economist & philosopher Friedrich Hayek and others proposed in 1938 a new liberal economic system with the name "neo-liberalism". Hayek argued that the **ONLY** purpose of governments was to remove all barriers to free economic activity. Deliberating with other intellectuals & academics over a period of years, the next landmark was the establishment of the Mont Pelerin Society in 1947. By this time, Keynesian economics was widely practised worldwide. The society was united in a belief that individual freedom was under threat from such policies. They wrote:

> *"The central values of civilization are in danger. This group´s object is solely, by facilitating the exchange of views among minds inspired by certain ideals and broad conceptions held in common, to contribute to the preservation and improvement of the free society."*[10]

---

10. Harvey, David, 'Freedom's Just Another Word…', *A Brief History of Neoliberalism* (Oxford, 2005; online edn, Oxford Academic, 12 Nov. 2020), <https://doi.org/10.1093/oso/9780199283262.003.0005>.

The idea of freedom from democratic control was central to their aims and continues to this day.

The group spent decades nurturing the concept until events of the 1970s provided them the opportunity to bring their ideas into the mainstream. This decade saw in the UK the collapse of manufacturing, widespread strikes, 20% mortgage rate, high unemployment, inflation above 10% and a 300% price rise of consumer goods. The 1978-79 "winter of discontent" paved the way for the election of Margaret Thatcher as prime minister in 1979. The Iron Lady was a disciple of Friedrich Hayek and was reported to have slammed down a copy of Hayek´s "The Constitution of Liberty" onto the cabinet table, stridently proclaiming: "*THIS is what we believe in!* ".

Over the period of her premiership, Mrs Thatcher instigated sweeping reforms based on Hayek´s ideas, including changes to the currency exchange rate mechanism (ushering in the age of globalisation), the transfer of state/public owned assets into the private sector and, importantly, deregulation of the financial sector; paving the way for the financial crash of 2008, resulting in austerity and a strengthening of neoliberal principles.

It is important to note that neoliberalism and the power of financial corporations have become not just a policy of government, but now take precedence over democratic processes. For example, corporations can sue governments for climate change policies that threaten their profits, receiving financial compensation at the taxpayer´s expense. Privatised water companies pay millions to their shareholders while polluting our rivers and waterways with raw sewage; sanctioned by government.

Many, perhaps the majority, believe that we are governed by a system of democracy. We aren´t. Virtually all areas of collective life throughout the world are now governed by the values of "the market" and those that control the markets. At the same time, key legislative protections, of the environment and human rights, are being attacked and dismantled because not considered conducive to economic growth & perceived prosperity. A multiplicity of factors; plastics pollution, environmental destruction, the health of our rivers & seas and of course climate change, to name but a very few, persist simply because the corporations responsible for these put the pursuit of financial profit & growth above all other considerations. Basic human needs such as housing, food, energy and gender equality are progressing out of reach of many, while bankers & financiers profit to obscene levels. Meanwhile the masses of people are "locked in" to this system, often finding themselves in a situation akin to modern slavery; unhappily labouring at boring, meaningless, increasingly insecure work, just to pay the rent, with the prospect of a big lottery win the only envisaged escape route.

Many believe that the current economic system is unsustainable and doomed to fail. What then would a viable alternative look like? UK economist Kate Raworth has summarised all the key issues to devise her radical model of Doughnut Economics. Just as Adam Smith, Keynes, Hayek, the Neoliberals & Margaret Thatcher devised their models to address the perceived challenges of their day, so Kate´s model addresses the challenges and social needs of ours. The doughnut envisages a **safe space** for economic development, between the needs of the planet & nature on the one hand and the needs of humans on the other.

It´s a simple yet revolutionary idea. As Kate explains: "Humanity´s 21st century challenge is to meet the needs of all within the means of the planet. In other words, to ensure that no one falls short on life´s essentials (from food and housing to healthcare and political voice), while ensuring that collectively we do not overshoot our pressure on Earth´s life-supporting systems, on which we fundamentally depend; such as a stable climate, fertile soils, and a protective ozone layer. The Doughnut of social and planetary boundaries is a playfully serious approach to framing that challenge, and it acts as a compass for human progress this century."

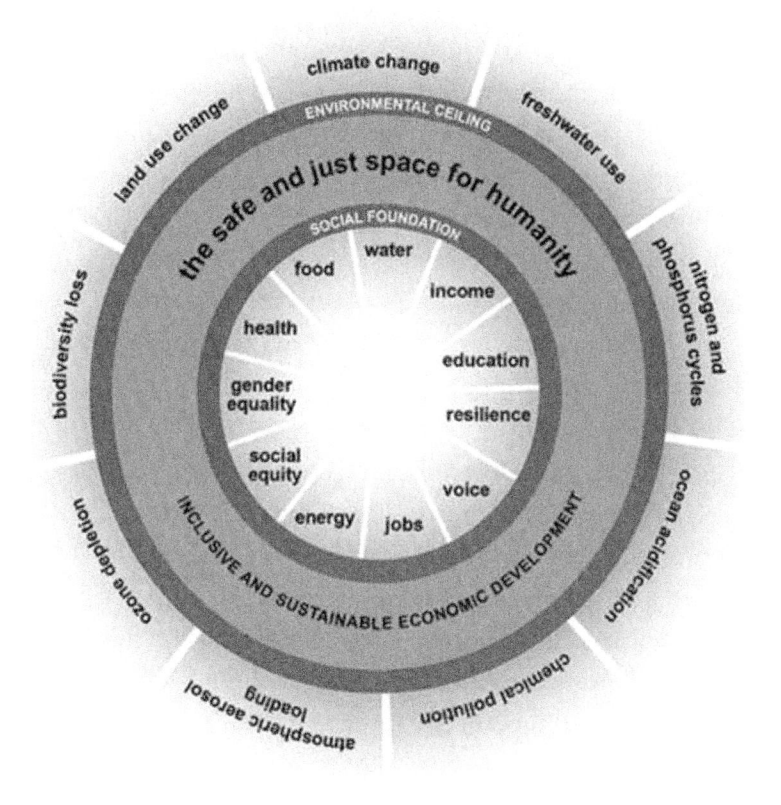

Proponents of the virtues of totally free market economics, often point to the ideas of Charles Darwin (1809-1882), founder of the Theory of Evolution, to justify their practices. Darwin's identification of the "survival of the fittest" as a key driver of human evolution is framed to somehow indicate that personal economic success, the accumulation of wealth through competition, is a good thing, natural and beneficial to humanity as a whole. Part of the enduring support to maintaining the current economic system is that it offers the prospect that, if you work hard and do your bit, you too can become one of the "winners" in the game of life. As we've seen, while there may well be individual winners, increasing numbers of people are losing assets of great value; their well-being, a clean healthy environment and, as climate change accelerates, even the ability to sustain their life. As Adam Smith himself enunciated it: "For one very rich man there must be at least five hundred poor." [11]

The evident evolution of human co-operation & altruism has always posed somewhat of a challenge to evolutionary biologists since the time of Darwin. It doesn't fit within the classical theory of evolution. The solutions to this dilemma all revolve around the idea that co-operation may not in theory benefit a single individual, but it certainly favours a massive magnification of collective interest. Which of course has benefit to every one of us. In fact, it's not just within the human realm that this can be observed. While natural selection through survival of the fittest is self-evident throughout nature at the individual level, equally demonstrable is the way that plants and animals co-

---

[11]. Online Library of Liberty: Adam Smith on Inequality Between the Rich and the Poor. Found in "An Inquiry Into the Nature and Causes of the Wealth of Nations (Cannan ed.), vol2. < https://oll.libertyfund.org/quote/adam-smith-inequality-rich-and-poor>

operate together symbiotically in their collective interest. It makes sense that the preservation of a healthy environment and abundant supply of food is in the best interests of all. Modern evolutionary theory has it that co-operation in nature has been a core component ever since single celled organisms first evolved into multi-cellular beings. This hypothesis was first proposed in 1967 by US biologist Lynn Margulis,[12] who endured years of ridicule from the scientific establishment before her insight was finally accepted.

At the moment there is a clear correlation between the principles informing the global economy and escalating catastrophic damage to the environment and human well-being. This understanding leads some to propose the adoption or enforcement of a socialist system, while others maintain that it is only by magnifying economic growth within the current system that the needed resources can be created. What is actually needed is a worldwide co-operative effort to halt the damage being caused, to repair that damage and to instigate some form of "new world order" in which that damage no longer occurs. It's not hard to understand a primary obstacle to achieving this when, according to Adam Smith, the very basis of most economic thinking relies on the fixed and apparently immutable belief that "self-interest and competition lead to economic prosperity".

---

12. Further Information: Nasa Science: Lynn Margulis.
<https://science.nasa.gov/people/lynn-margulis/>

> "He who controls the money supply of a nation controls the nation." James A Garfield [13]

A fundamental shift to an economy that has as its primary aim collective interest for nature and human well-being, and the needed co-operation to achieve this, is made much easier if we look at the way that the money supply has changed over the centuries leading to the current transitional era. Beginning with barter, followed by the minting of gold, paper currency linked to gold and finally free-standing currencies simply linked to each other, the understanding of what money and financial transactions essentially are has undergone several revolutionary changes. Founded in 1851, the New York and Mississippi Valley Printing Telegraph Company, later known as Western Union, could be thought of as a precursor of the internet. Dominating the American telegraphy industry until quite recently, in 1860 it facilitated the first electronic transfer of money. From this point on, the world has slowly transitioned into the era of electronic money.

In 1949, a New York businessman, Frank McNamara, had been entertaining potential new clients at an upmarket restaurant. When it came time to pay the bill, he was embarrassed to discover that he'd left his wallet

---

13. James Garfield, 20th US President, elected 1880, assassinated 200 days later. Further information <https://www.whitehouse.gov/about-the-white-house/presidents/james-garfield/>

at home. Fortunately, his wife was able to pay the bill and the new clients weren't lost. However, it gave Frank the brilliant idea of creating the Diners Club, issuing a plastic card with which the first 200 members could pay for meals at selected restaurants; with a small fee charged on each transaction. From what was basically the first credit card, it took another 10 years for American Express to issue their credit card, followed by others before the credit/debit card system became entrenched as it is today. It's a very astute business idea; charging people more money to spend their money and creating a good earner for the banks. The next step came in 1999 when European banks introduced mobile banking through computer devices. By 2017, the majority of financial transactions worldwide were in the form of purely digital transactions. No cash, no cards, just information in a vast global computer programme.

This form of currency, fiat money, has no value in relationship to anything else. Its only value is a "collective agreement" that it has value. That value is based on debt. For example, if you want to make a large purchase, like a new car or a house, the chances are that you won't have the cash in your bank account. Most likely you will need to take out a loan or mortgage and so you engage the services of a lender who will loan you the money, to be repaid at interest. Actually, that's not strictly true. There isn't a pot of money held by these lender institutions that they can dip into. Rather, new money is created by, in the UK the Bank of England, and loaned to the lender institution at interest, who in turn loans it to you at a greater level of interest; all achieved by multiple punches of computer keyboards. The net result is that now, more debt has been created than money exists to repay that debt. It applies both to you personally and also the lenders who facilitated the loan or mortgage. For this reason, the system can only continue if linked to the need to create unending economic growth, with all the damage that that causes to nature and humanity. For human beings, it propagates a lifestyle that has to be focussed on the accumulation of money by whatever means, rather than opening up the pursuit of individual fulfilment or activities to benefit the whole. "I'd love to be doing X, but I can't because I need the money." In addition, the vast mountain of debt created by the system is considered a financial asset in its own right, as a global network of financiers, bankers & investors trade in this debt, with enormous sums to be made on the backs of us all. Lots more activity sitting in front of a screen! It's a vicious cycle, not confined to individual debt. It also applies to governments. We are led to believe that the provision of government led public services is paid for through taxation. Wrong. Again, new money for services is simply created by the Bank of England and loaned to the government. Your taxes go towards paying back the loan... plus interest.

It wouldn't be so bad if the system was stable and

supported a stable civil society. But it doesn't. On 15 September 2008 the investment bank Lehman Brothers collapsed, sending shockwaves through the global financial system and beyond. The root cause of this was the so-called sub-prime mortgage scandal in the US, whereby many mortgages were given that it was not possible to repay; predatory behaviour of the rich exploiting the poor. As described above, investors had traded in these debts and led to the collapse. In the UK, the contagion first led to Northern Rock and from then to the other high street banks. The then chancellor of the exchequer, Alistair Darling, in a BBC documentary [14] described meeting with the heads of UK banks and being informed that they were rapidly approaching a situation where neither cashpoint machines nor debit/credit cards would work anymore. In other words, when no-one could buy anything or get any money. When asked how long it might take before this happened, the answer was "about 4 hours". While we survived that, not least due to a massive government cash injection of £137 billion (repaid through years of austerity and a catastrophic decline of public services), the basic principles of the current economic system remain largely unchanged. Except of course that the rich have got richer, the poor have got poorer and the range of available work is more and more confined to whatever will make money, rather than what is of true value.

---

14. BBC2: The Bank That Almost Broke Britain.

It doesn't have to be like this. Because money is now simply created by a keystroke on a computer terminal, the amount of money available is theoretically unlimited... **IF** released from the burden of interest payments. This understanding is the basis for a current (2023) two-year trial in the UK of Universal Basic Income (UBI). UBI is a concept where every adult is given a monthly sum of money to live on, irrespective of their wealth level or employment status. Piloted in two locations, central Jarrow in north-east England and East Finchley in north London, the monthly sum has been set at £1600. Previous trials of UBI throughout the world, have yielded interesting results. As well as eradicating poverty, the stigma of unemployment and allegations of "welfare scrounging", it has created a profound shift in the lifestyles of participants. Rather than settling into laziness, people tend to gravitate towards two things; the pursuit of vocational interests and voluntary work for the benefit of the community. Most importantly, it eradicates the universal worry about not having enough to live on. It could be, if we so choose, a key component in the transition from the economic/social system instigated by the industrial revolution.

The global cost of attaining net zero carbon dioxide emissions has been put at 125 trillion dollars. This is a staggering sum and probably unachievable within the present economic system. However, that sum is available if the money supply is liberated from those who have a vested financial interest in the creation & maintenance of unsustainable debt. Such a move would immediately re-invent the banking and money supply system back to its original founding purpose: to 'promote the public Good and Benefit of our People'.

But would the present system of governance agree to this?

Chapter 4

Politics & Governance

"Revolt is the right of the people". John Locke (1632-1704).

The ancient Greek city of Athens lived under a radical form of government from 508 until 322 BC, giving to the world and future generations the enduring concept of "democracy"; the word deriving from *demos* (the people) and *kratos* (force or power). It literally means "people power". Unlike today, where local and national democratic governance, following the pattern established by John Locke, consists of the election of representatives to make decisions on our behalf, in ancient Athens the people governed themselves; debating, deliberating and voting on issues and laws great and small affecting their community, through regular meetings of the *Assembly*. All male adult citizens (excluding slaves) were entitled to speak, express their opinion, and vote within the assembly. While the system was open to criticism, the Athenians understood the value of checks, balances and strict procedures to avoid the deliberations of the Assembly descending into chaos, corruption and anarchy. In parallel to the Assembly, the ultimate seat of power, were 2 other institutions: the *Council* and the *Legislature*. The Council consisted of 500 citizens who were appointed to serve for just 1 year and were paid. Its main functions were to prepare the agenda for the Assembly of citizens to deliberate and vote on, and to enact it´s decisions. The Legislature administered Laws. Laws were considered to be the ultimate governing principle. They applied to all people without exception and regardless of their wealth or status. Laws could be changed through the Assembly, but only by proposing and voting through a new law to replace an existing one.

The democratic system was introduced to replace a prior Greek system where governance was administered solely by those in possession of wealth. The history of democracy in ancient Greece, and in fact ever since, bore witness to a struggle & conflict of interest between these two groupings; the people and the oligarchy. Periodically, the oligarchy assumed control in order to retain their power, only for it then to be returned to the people. Paralleling these political reforms, there were also measures to cancel debts, free imprisoned debtors and changing the rules on borrowing to avoid debt. The ancient Greeks were dealing with exactly the same political-economic issues that have characterised societies up to the present day. It can be truly said that the more things change, the more they stay the same. In contrast to then, our present political system bears distinct similarities, as well as differences. While we have a form of democracy, our voice is reduced to the unsatisfactory option of, every few years, choosing from a small handful of individuals to make decisions for us. Often the choice is reduced to a perceived "lesser of two evils" rather than someone who truly represents our personal beliefs and ideas for the greater good. Any vote cast for a fringe candidate who does appear to be representing a more ethical value system is a wasted vote under the present "first past the post" system. Once elected, they do exactly what they want to do and we are powerless to stop them. A recent YouGov poll[15] showed that only 10% of voters now believe that mainstream politicians act in the public interest; a figure that has been in continual decline since the 1940s. A staggering 78% claim that politicians' principle concern is either themselves, the interests of their financial backers or their particular ideology/party winning/retaining power, rather than the concerns of the electorate who voted for them. Not only have we lost confidence in politicians to perform the function that we deserve, it appears that the system itself is also losing our belief in its effectiveness & integrity.

US president & founding father Thomas Jefferson (1743-1826) said that: "*The care of human life and happiness, and*

---

15. YouGov: "Political disaffection is rising and driving UKIP support". < https://yougov.co.uk/politics/articles/10820>

not their destruction, is the first and only object of good government."[16] While we may all have varied ideas about how to achieve this, the principle itself is surely not in question. Neither is a broad consensus that the representative democratic political establishment has somehow lost it. While many believe that these problems could be solved if only we could elect into power the right people, perhaps it is the system itself that is now the problem. Governance, and our systems for delivering it, have always been an evolving process, changing over the centuries as our understanding of essential human needs change and our ability to meet those needs also change. This has produced a basic division of political ideology between "right" and "left". Throughout the political discourse, opposing sides have become embroiled and consumed by the hate-filled narrative that we, right or left, leaver or remainer, people like us not them, and many other divisions, are not only right in our actions and beliefs and the other side wrong, but actually the other side, human beings just like us, are EVIL; a recipe for global war. Both sides blame the other for the ills of society; producing tribalism and an increasingly bitter and hostile social environment. To add further fuel to this tragic situation, mainstream politicians, and their media allies on all sides, deliberately & actively provoke these divisions to foster their own narrow ambition and self-interest.

16.Founders Online: "Thomas Jefferson to the Republicans of Washington County, Maryland, 31 March 1809". <
https://founders.archives.gov/documents/Jefferson/03-01-02-0088>

To introduce a further complication, since the 1960s, and rapidly gaining momentum, a new political division is emerging between those who view nature as an expendable resource to be economically exploited in the pursuit of both left & right agendas, and those who have a more "ecological" awareness of the intrinsic value of the natural world, and the need to protect, enhance and conserve it at all costs. This view has adherents across the entire political spectrum, but is still not represented as a majority political issue within our existing governance structure.

> *"When the proposal is made that we must continue what we are doing "in order to provide jobs" it must be considered as an unacceptable solution when a much greater abundance of jobs is available for repairing the already damaged environment. All our professions and institutions need to be reinvented in this new context. We must in a manner reinvent the human itself as a mode of being." From The Great Work by Thomas Berry* [17]

What a mess! The now perceived simplistic ideas of enlightenment thinkers Adam Smith & John Locke, the protection of property derived from self-interest & the exploitation of nature, have resulted in an escalating crisis, out of which there seems to be no escape. Indeed,

---

17. Berry, Thomas (ed.) (1999). The Great Work: Our Way Into the Future. Harmony.

as Locke put it: "There is no practical alternative to majority political rule, i.e., to taking the consent of the majority as the act of the whole and binding every individual. It would be next to impossible to obtain the consent of every individual before acting collectively ... No rational people could desire and constitute a society that had to dissolve straightaway because the majority was unable to make the final decision and the society was incapable of acting as one body."[18]

But would it? The ancient Greeks, Jefferson, Locke, and many other political philosophers over the centuries, all deliberated and theorised about a civil society bereft of the influence of arguably the most important product of the industrial revolution; the development of an internet based global communication system. Through this technology, we now have the ability to engage with any individual on the planet in possession of a smartphone, tablet or PC. Through this technology, we can receive live updates on current developments in any place on earth. We can visibly see and make judgements on the behaviour of any politicians anywhere. If we so choose, we can educate ourselves on the background factors behind any political event. We have the means to create alliances with any group and to vote on any issue. The technology throws into sharp relief exactly the type of

---

18. John Locke, Second Treatise, pp 95 – 99. < https://press-pubs.uchicago.edu/founders/documents/v1ch4s1.html>

universal situation that any kind of despotic ruler most fears; an educated, informed, empowered, aware people with the means to challenge their authority. The technology also provides those same rulers with a powerful weapon at their disposal; the ability to broadcast propaganda, misinformation and divisive rhetoric. The old political strategy of "divide and rule" still has many adherents, to the cost of us all.

In ancient Greece, the philosopher Plato (427-347 BC) described a 5-fold degeneration of democracy from the ideal of Rule by the Wise, through Rule by the Powerful, and ending in Tyranny.[19] For the multitudes who despair at the inaction of government, both local and national, in the face of accelerating global catastrophe, maybe that point of tyrannical inaction & indecisiveness has now been reached. Plato is widely regarded as the most significant political theorist in history. His ideas are well worth revisiting to gain insight on our current predicament. He believed that all the many conflicting interests & viewpoints within society could be brought into harmony through a political order that allowed all people to flourish. Born into a family of rulers on both his mother's and father's side, in early life he assumed that he would have a career as a politician. However, it was not to be, finding himself unable to identify with either any of the existing political parties, or the

---

19. Jeremy Reid, Plato on Democracy, San Francisco State University. <https://philarchive.org/archive/REIPOD-2>

corruption within the political establishment of the time. Instead he became an academic, working within *The Academy*, his own creation and, in effect, the world's first university.

He believed that the most important issue in politics is not policy as such, rather the nature of the political order. For Plato, simply being guided by public opinion is not the best way to make decisions. Public opinion can be too easily manipulated by the self-interests of the media, the loudest and apparently most convincing voices, with little understanding given to learning the lessons of history. Instead, Plato elevates the concept of "justice" as central to his vision. The subject of almost continual philosophical debate as to its nature ever since, Plato argues that the best definition of justice in the political order is not to the advantage of any particular faction or group in society. Rather, it concerns the well-being and the common good of the whole political order.

In trying to define what sort of political order best serves the whole, Plato points to a basic fundamental & unchanging truth of society; that there is social diversity and conflicting interests between different groups. Furthermore he argued that, because appealing to one groups interests over another can only ever lead to disharmony & strife, the best political order is one based on creating peace & goodwill, friendship and co-operation between different people, valuing each other and the contributions all bring to the common good.[20]

In other words, the complete opposite of our current political order! The basic strategy of many politicians today seeking election can be summarised as: "Candidate B is a rotten ignorant scumbag. Vote for me and every day will be the first day of spring." Not merely uncivilised, but also wrong. The vast majority of would-be politicians begin with the best of intentions; the ideal of public service for the perceived common good. However, once elected they might rapidly find themselves embroiled within a system that is anything but. Instead intrigue, factionalism, strategic manoeuvring and outright lying become the order of the day; an environment in which fondly held ideals rapidly disintegrate when confronted with the "real world". The available options are often now reduced to a) resign in order to spend more time with the family, b) have a nervous breakdown and self-medicate, or c) avail oneself of the financial & other opportunities that now come my way. The news media can confirm that many politicians choose these routes, especially the latter.

A different slant on this can be found in the work of Larry Diamond (born 1951). A US citizen, Diamond is widely regarded as the leading contemporary academic in the field of democracy studies. Like Plato and Locke

---

20. Internet Encyclopedia of Philosophy. Plato: Political Philosophy. <https://iep.utm.edu/platopol/>

before him, he regards the structure and functioning of governance to be the most pressing issue to be addressed in the world today, specifically stressing that it must be improved in nations already practicing democratic systems. As he states: "for democratic structures to endure – and be worthy of endurance – they must listen to their citizens' voices, engage their participation, tolerate their protests, protect their freedoms, and respond to their needs."[21] He defines modern democracy to consist of four essential elements: a political system for choosing and replacing the government through free and fair elections, the active participation of citizens in politics and civic life, protection of the human rights of all citizens and the rule of law - in which laws and procedures apply equally to all citizens.

We have the first of Diamonds four elements, although, especially in the US through the figure of Trump, and also elsewhere in the democratic world, the "fair" principle is beginning to be questioned. This might also extend to his second element. While the internet and the news media certainly massively enable the active participation of citizens in the political discourse, doubts can be raised about the integrity of information received. The internet & social media is well-known as a vehicle for the propagation of "fake news" designed to whip up a response of outrage, while the advent of artificial

---

21. Diamond, Larry (2008). *The Spirit of Democracy: The Struggle to Build Free Societies Throughout the World.* New York: Henry Holt and Company, LLC

intelligence makes possible the creation of faked recordings, audio or video, of public figures speaking; the content of which is completely falsified, in order to generate hostility. As for the other two elements, we are now in an era where legislation to protect human rights is being increasingly ignored & undermined by democratically elected governments; themselves increasingly the recipient of legal challenges to certain policies. One clue as to why this should be so might be found in the discussion about the new Neoliberal economic order in the previous chapter. Here it was noted that a core requirement of neoliberalism, the dominant economic ideology in the world today, is a release from the moderating influence of political democracy.

Whichever way you look at it, representative democracy appears to be increasingly under threat. The question becomes one of how Plato's ideal political order of peace, justice, goodwill, friendship and co-operation might become realised within the internet era. One response to this might be to declare that it can't, due to human nature. This point will be addressed in the final chapter 7. Another response is to look at the basic facts of the current global order. As well as the fact of the internet, a world-wide web connecting us all together, we also live within an integrated planetary economic system. The scientifically proven facts of the environmental and climate crises remind us that on an organic biological level also, the world is a single entity. In all ways, bar one, we are a unified global entity. If you travel out into space, an adventure that is the preserve of a privileged few, the same thing can be seen. One such, US astronaut Edgar Mitchell, couldn't have put it any better:

> *"You develop an instant global consciousness, a people orientation, an intense dissatisfaction with the state of the world, and a compulsion to do something about it. From out there on the moon, international politics look so petty. You want to grab a politician by the scruff of the neck and drag him a quarter of a million miles out and say, 'Look at that, you son of a bitch."*

The one exception to the reality of "One World" is the domain of governance, specifically the way that the primary structure of current global politics derives from the separation of humanity into nation states. At one time this structure might have been defined by ethnicity. However, another factor of the one world, global transport & migration, has brought us to a position where people of all ethnicities can be found living in every nation on earth. Further, much to the disdain of nationalists, ethnic & familial relationships often assume a greater significance within the individual identity than does the nation in which he/she happens to currently live. Tragically, this can also be a source of profound conflict; within the individual, within the nation and between nations.

Nationhood, as both a political entity and also a psychological orientation, is the product of previous historical transitions, as discussed in chapter 1; before the world was recognised as one. Most wars, with the exception of ethnically based civil wars, are between nations; often fought not just for resources or territory, but for the prestige of the nation. Despite the "one world" economic system in which we live, the viability of political leaders is most often determined by the condition of the separate national economy. People fall out if they happen to display the wrong flag and national flags are the essential prop to any televised interview with a politician. Look at any map of the world and it most often displays national, rather than bio-ecological boundaries. In all ways, our habitual orientation to the world is guided by nationalism; the division of both humanity and the natural world into nations with national governments. Is it inconceivable that the future world might one day look back on all this, with all the problems and conflicts it engenders, as nothing more than a passing phase?

If that is the case, the embryonic beginnings of a new transition into sustainability in the realm of governance might be found in two apparently contradictory, but actually complementary, movements: Localism & Globalism. Both seek to fulfil the visions of the ideal civic order as defined by the aforementioned political philosophers and both are beginning to happen now.

Within the UK, representative democracy is stratified between the national government, local authorities, county councils or unitary authorities, town councils and the smallest unit, only in some places, of parish councils. All practice the election of representatives. With the exception of the latter, all operate on a practical level through an unelected bureaucracy of civil servants, council officers and such like. Often, the practical day to day decisions are made by these bodies, rather than the elected members. For citizens, they are out of reach, immune to direct approaches and communicate only with the elected representatives.

A quick Google search on "local authority culture of bullying" reveals a horrifying pattern throughout the entire UK. Extensively documented and of widespread concern, this same culture ensues within many governmental working environments, as well as other public services including the NHS; an aggressive and bullying style of hierarchical line management that rewards ruthless ambition while suppressing well-being, truthfulness, healthy debate and innovation. It engenders fear, paranoia and mental illness, much whispering in small groups and the ever-present dominant need to watch ones back. Misogyny is widespread & endemic. Whistle-blowers, revealing malpractice, are routinely intimidated and silenced, while truly conscientious individuals often feel they have little option but to resign and pursue livelihood in a more humane environment, if they aren't sacked first. Little wonder then that us, the people, the ones who pay their wages through our taxes, who might feel dependent on their intervention, are often regarded as a nuisance; an irritation to be fobbed off and avoided at all costs.

In reality, the political process starts with the local community itself. For most people, the issues that they want politicians to address are those that affect them personally and directly. The Local Government Association now recognises that communities benefit directly from greater involvement in the way local services are delivered, citing 19 specific advantages on issues that the current system is increasingly struggling with, including enhancing well-being, reducing costs and improving services.[22] But isn´t this what we want politicians to do, and recognise that they are failing to do? The implication is clear: everyone benefits when political power is restored to communities. By a system of electing politicians to act on our behalf, the reverse happens and the ability to influence public services is actually removed from communities; producing disillusionment, discontent and disinterest.

When the pandemic struck, and ever since, the news media was and still is full of the struggles and conflicts

---

22. Local Government Association. Local.gov.uk

within the government response. These conflicts included arguments between politicians and health professionals, concerns from the public about the appropriateness of the response, and valid questions about the way that public money was being corruptly syphoned off to incompetent providers of healthcare equipment; especially when they turned out to be personal friends or financial supporters of MPs. Contrast this with what actually happened within communities, as friends and neighbours rallied around to support the old and vulnerable; making sure everyone had food and comfort. As so often when a crisis strikes, communities turned inwards in a natural display of solidarity and goodwill. It almost seems like we are naturally wired to act in this way. The local community shows how it should be done; a practical demonstration of Plato's vision of the ideal civic society demonstrating "goodwill, friendship and co-operation between different people".

The representative democratic system is founded on one glaring error; the idea that a single person has enough wisdom, empathy and altruism to act in everyone's best interests. In reality, no one individual, organisation or political perspective has all the solutions to all the problems and challenges that we collectively face at all levels of our community life. However, the whole community itself; the collective summation of interests, intelligence, skills, perspectives and experience of all community members, most definitely does have. It might be next to impossible to practice this at the level of national or local authority governance, but it can be manifested at the local neighbourhood level.

Localism is a growing political philosophy that recognises the local community as a political entity; emphasising the value of the local economy, local history, local connections & relationships and local autonomy. The Localism Act (2011), introduced by the government of David Cameron under his "big society" initiative, enshrines many principles of this philosophy into legal form. Significantly, section 81 of the act states that a "relevant authority" (county or district council) **MUST** consider an "expression of interest" by a "relevant body… in providing or assisting in providing a relevant service on behalf of the authority". The Act states that a relevant body can be a community group.[23] The implications of this are profound, suggesting that a neighbourhood group of local residents can take over the functions of local government. These might include the provision of services and the levy & spending of a local taxation system.

Whoa… now hang on! If your local neighbourhood is anything like mine, there are people around here that I definitely wouldn't trust to do this. If you're concerned

---

23. Localism Act (2011), Section 81:
<https://www.legislation.gov.uk/ukpga/2011/20/section/81/enacted>

about the ethics & values of national politicians, you'd be horrified at the way that some in our local parish council behave! Fortunately, there is another alternative that is coming into current perspective. The Electoral Reform Society has done much work on the development of citizen's assemblies as a new form of governance structure.

> *"With the support of the Economic and Social Research Council, academics and civil society organisations brought together politicians, regional leaders and the public to debate a range of options for Britain's constitutional future. Between October and November 2015, two pilot [citizens] assemblies were run to ask how new regional powers can be established in a form that is supported by the people who live locally. In November 2016, the Democracy Matters Citizens' Assembly project won a Democratic Innovation Award at the Political Studies Association Annual Awards in Westminster. Deliberative approaches, such as citizen assemblies, lend themselves to providing answers to questions of decentralisation, devolution and democracy. They emphasise two key aspects of democracy: first, participation of ordinary citizens who are affected by the decision, not just members of the political elite; and, second, careful discussion that builds deep understanding of the options and the arguments for and against them."*[24]

---

24. citizensassembly.co.uk

The role and structure of citizens assemblies is a topical current subject. However, growing in parallel to this is the concept of the Neighbourhood Assembly of all citizens. Open to all local citizens and carrying out its function of deliberation via the internet, it is the nearest modern equivalent to the ancient Greek system of democracy. And of course, unlike the Greek assembly, it includes women! Its neither inconceivable nor impractical to suggest that this idea could develop into a new form of democratic governance.

Citizens or Neighbourhood Assemblies can work well at the local level. The emphasis on the value of deliberation is crucial, as well as the potential of the internet to enable direct democracy; a whole community vote on specific issues. At the global level, we are confronted with the reality that, in lots of ways, some sort of world government might be an appropriate response to the many current issues that have a transnational perspective; a harmonising body that reconciles the many different national self-interests. The subject of many conspiracy theories, the topic of a "new world order" is a somewhat frightening prospect. The basic conspiracy theory outlines the idea of a shadowy elite of people secretly pulling the strings to establish a global totalitarian authority. Some variants of the theory attribute it to the disciples of the antichrist. Other less controversial elements point to the machinations of international neoliberal financiers. There may well be a strong element of truth to this. However, there is another factual tradition of events that point to a very different kind of world government.

The inevitable result of a world of separate nation states in competition with each other, combined with the predilections of some to deliberately stir things up, inevitably leads to armed conflict, with all the horrors that that involves. Thus it was that World One 1 erupted in 1914, producing a bitter harvest of 5 million civilian deaths, 23 million wounded and 9 million dead soldiers. The main result after 4 years was that some nations states ceased to exist, and new ones were created. Over a hundred years later, arguments still rage about whether the deaths were heroic acts of sacrifice to create a better world, or a futile waste of human life to try and resolve the arguments of just a handful of individuals. However, one major outcome was the founding of the League of Nations in 1920; the world's first transnational organisation with a strict purpose to preserve peace. A major goal of the League was to resolve international disputes by a process of negotiation and arbitration, rather than slaughtering young men & innocent civilians. It also had a mandate to address other global humanitarian concerns including just treatment of minorities, drug trafficking, the arms trade and global health issues. What it didn't do was address one of the root causes of world conflict; the very existence of separate nation states. The United States never joined the

League, while Germany, Italy and Japan all dropped out in the 1930s. I wonder why?

The reason of course was that they still preferred the old way, and hence 1939 saw the outbreak of World War 2. The newer weapons of mass destruction developed since the first war, resulted in a vast increase in the numbers of avoidable deaths; an estimated 75 million this time. That's a 600% increase. The ultimate transitional moment that effectively brought it to an end was of course the US nuclear bombing of the Japanese cities of Hiroshima & Nagasaki. One moment of unbelievable human cruelty brought a swift death to between 129,000 and 226,000 innocent civilians and introduced a new era of fear into human awareness. To date 2 nuclear weapons have been used and 12,500 are sitting ready to be used.

While many still anticipate that the continuing & escalating incidence of armed conflict between nations & different ethnic groups will possibly lead to World War 3, one result of the second world war, and the failure of the League of Nations to prevent it, led to the founding of the United Nations in 1945, with the same basic purpose. Currently, it is the largest organisation on the planet. The UN Declaration of Universal Human Rights[25] is a comprehensive statement of humanitarian

---

25. Full Text: < https://www.un.org/en/about-us/universal-declaration-of-human-rights>

principles concerning all people. The overall umbrella organisation consists of a vast range of specialised agencies, including NGOs (non-governmental organisations), 15 organisations dedicated to various transnational issues, and elects judges to the International Court of Justice. This latter adjudicates on matters of international law, including the genocide convention. A new potential area of jurisdiction of the court stems from the life's work of Scottish lawyer Polly Higgins (1968-2019). Founder of the Earth Law Alliance, Polly's contribution to the sustainability transition was to campaign for Ecocide, the destruction of natural ecosystems, to be recognised as a crime against humanity.

The attitude of humanity towards the United Nations ranges from a belief in it as the most important force for peace & human development in the world today... to dismissal of it as biased, corrupt and ineffective. The UN is currently the closest thing we have today to a form of world government. The name, "united nations", embodies a powerful symbolic statement of intent. Its deficiencies derive in part from the fact that it is still controlled & manipulated by separate nation states, with representatives appointed by national governments.

This chapter has pointed to a number of issues coming into focus as representing elements of a global transition in the field of politics & governance; including proportional representation, citizens assemblies, localism, direct democracy and a reformed united nations. All currently are considered within the context of governance being a system inherited from previous transitions, and inseparable from increasingly globalised economic systems; themselves a product partly of scientific and technological progress. All are also integrated within a scientific understanding of what we actually are; the human element within the cosmos. The Industrial Revolution was and is still a scientific revolution; the subject of the next chapter.

Chapter 5

Science: Entry into a New Reality

As the tram passed the grand clock in the town square, Albert's heart sank as he contemplated the tedium and difficulty of yet another day ahead at his menial desk job in the patent office. There must be more to life than this, he thought. It would be another four hours before he would be able to enjoy the lunch of sandwiches lovingly prepared by his wife: Mrs Einstein. If only there was a way to speed up the day! He looked again at the clock. What if this tram was travelling much faster? I mean really fast; at a speed approaching the velocity of light itself? Immediately, the cares of the coming day receded as his creative imagination swung into action; visualising the tram speeding away from the clock, visualising rays of light moving from the clock into his eye, visualising the amended movements of the clock hands that would now ensue…

The ability to visualise simultaneous complex multi-dimensional mind pictures, is just one of a number of special and unique abilities possessed by many people with dyslexia. It would be several years before this ability would establish Albert Einstein's reputation as arguably the greatest scientist of the twentieth century. What is not so well known is that throughout his life he struggled to write legibly, preferring the language of numbers. He had great difficulty with reading and could only read at all if he was able to translate the words on the page into a picture in his mind. In fact, in addition to the scientific ideas for which he is well known, Einstein also reported extensively on the unique way that his cognition worked to perform, with great difficulty, many of the linguistic tasks that most non-dyslexic people take for granted.

Just like Sir Isaac Newton before him, Einstein was a genius but also with, shall we say, certain difficulties which set him apart. Those difficulties were clearly manifest from an early age. As a young child, he began to talk very late; a situation that compelled his worried parents to seek medical advice. He hated school, and from all accounts the feeling was mutual. One teacher told him that he would be much happier if he, Einstein, wasn't in his class at all, adding that he was disrespectful and would never achieve anything in life. Perhaps the problem was the school system itself. The current UK schools National Curriculum for Mathematics states that "These are the statutory programmes of study and attainment targets for mathematics at key stages 1 to 4.

They are issued by law; <u>you must follow them</u> unless there's a good reason not to. All schools maintained by the local authority in England <u>must teach these programmes</u> of study from September 2016" [26]. Let's take an example. At age 12, Key stage 4 determines that students understand and use place value for decimals, measures and integers of any size. Basic stuff. However, at this age, Einstein had taught himself Euclidean geometry in the school holiday, independently discovered his own original proof of Pythagoras' Theorem and started learning differential calculus, which he had mastered by age 14. And that's not all. In his spare time, he became enamoured of enlightenment thinker Immanuel Kant's "Critique of Pure Reason"[27]; a tome routinely described as incomprehensible to mere mortals. All this, and much more, occurred before he was expelled at age 16 for a "bad attitude".

It could be that he managed to achieve universally recognised excellence in life in spite of, not because of, his dyslexia? The condition of dyslexia was first identified by a British ophthalmologist W. Pringle

---

26. UK National Curriculum for Mathematics < https://www.gov.uk/government/publications/national-curriculum-in-england-mathematics-programmes-of-study>

27. Immanuel Kant (1724-1804), "*Critique of Pure Reason*", first published 1781 and in print ever since. The book essentially deals with the way that we derive knowledge of the world through 2 sources; the senses and understanding. While elevating the principle of reason, Kant states that it can't know everything.

Morgan in 1896. He described a 14-year-old boy, Percy, who despite intensive tuition, drilling and practice over a number of years, stubbornly demonstrated an inability to spell his own name correctly, also consistently failing to write the "P" of Percy properly. The letter might appear as a "d" or a "b" on diverse occasions. While it was not uncommon to find individuals failing to master these types of skills, what was unusual in this case was that Percy was immediately recognisable to his teachers, by a very long way, as the most intelligent and gifted pupil in the school.

Percy? Einstein? In fact, Isaac Newton himself is now reckoned to have been not only dyslexic, but also suffering with ADHD (attention deficit hyperactive disorder) and Aspergers Syndrome; a condition on the autistic spectrum. We now regard the "scientific method" as a 4-stage process of 1) coming up with a theory about something 2) devising an experiment to test that theory 3) observing the results of that experiment and 4) drawing a conclusion. Let's begin by suggesting a theory, something along the lines of; "dyslexia is not so much a disability, rather a unique way of thinking 'outside the box' that makes possible the discovery of new things". The suggested experiment is to examine the history of great scientific discoveries and see if dyslexia is present in the people making those discoveries. The results are interesting to say the least and contain some well-known names.

- Leonardo da Vinci: painter, designer, scientist, futurist and thinker. Dyslexic.
- Galileo: discovered the sun, rather than the earth, to be the centre of the solar system. Dyslexic.
- Alexander Graham Bell: the telephone. Dyslexic
- Thomas Edison: electric power generation, sound recording, motion pictures, the lightbulb. Dyslexic.
- Michael Faraday: electro-magnetic induction. Dyslexic
- The Wright Brothers: the aeroplane. Dyslexic.
- Wernher von Braun: rocket and space technology. Dyslexic.
- Steve Jobs: personal computer. Dyslexic.
- Stephen Hawkins: Gravitational & Spacetime Singularity. Dyslexic.

The list can go on and on, and includes not only lots of women, but also radical pioneers in many areas of life; core areas that have directly contributed to the world as we now know it and without which contemporary life would be very different. It's worth saying that for most of these people & many many more, their schooling, in which dyslexia is currently labelled as a "learning disability", was an obstacle rather than an encouragement to their later achievements in life. For Albert Einstein, the breakthrough came at age 16 when a well-connected family friend was able to persuade the Swiss Federal Institute of Technology to let him take the entrance exam. Despite being very young, well below the entrance age for the institute, and scoring poorly in most of the exam subjects, he achieved outstanding excellence in Physics and Maths. The rest is history, as at the Institute he entered an environment in which original thought was valued and nurtured rather than being feared and dismissed as indicating a dangerous inclination to subversion and rebelliousness.

It may be false to draw the conclusion that dyslexia is a necessary precursor to achieving excellence in the realm of science and technology. However, the ability to think things in a way that nobody else has been able to is a much more viable outcome to conclude; dyslexic or otherwise. The issue is that the school system seeks to standardise children, rather than to value originality and diversity; the very qualities that characterise human progress. Certainly, some sort of radical transition in our education system to support this might be needed. Currently, schooling is directed by the government as training to occupy a productive position within the economic system. The ideal product of this training is someone who will keep their mouth shut and do what they're told, rather than becoming a "whole, unique & integrated human being"; one theme of the final chapter 7 and a key element of the transition into sustainability. For school survivor Albert Einstein (1879-1955), his life's work became dedicated to a new understanding of the nature of time, space, matter and energy. The epitome of a 20th century caricature of the "mad scientist" with his wild hair-do, habit of a minimum 10 hours sleep a night (as well as regular naps throughout the day) and pathological hatred of wearing socks, many of his ideas are difficult to understand, to say the least. His well-known equation showing the equivalence of matter (M) and energy (E), $E=Mc^2$, has been described as the most famous equation in the world. As well as indicating the awesome destructive energy of nuclear weapons, for which Einstein reportedly said "*If I had known what they were going to do with it, I'd have become a shoemaker*", the equation also brought into popular awareness the speed of light (c). Standing at an incredible 186,000 miles per SECOND, it gives us an indication of just how incomprehensibly big the universe really is. The nearest star to us is about 4.24 light-years away, meaning that light travelling at that unbelievably fast speed takes over 4 years to get here. And that's just the nearest star of the estimated 200 billion trillion in existence. What must those first humans who discovered the use of fire have made of it if they could have understood what it was all leading to. Or as Einstein himself put it: "*Two things are infinite; the universe and human stupidity.*"

Prior to the 20th century, science and technology had followed a fairly predictable course. At each stage new discoveries had led to new technologies, which in turn led to new social & work patterns and adjustments to the majority lifestyle. At each stage, the new developments became integrated into the prevailing economic and political systems, facilitating progress without massively disrupting them too much. Sometimes, a major discovery, for instance learning that the earth is not the centre of the universe, conflicted with the prevailing religious orthodoxy of the day. For Galileo, challenging the teachings of the church meant house arrest for the last 8 years of his life. But we managed to live with his discovery. Following a brief turbulence, the status quo was reaffirmed and we moved on. However, beginning with Einstein in the 20th century, science, especially physics & the natural sciences, began to learn things which would very radically alter our whole conception of the nature of reality. The predictable, measurable, "universe as a giant machine" established by Isaac Newton has now been replaced by something very different and distinctly strange; demanding in turn a very different kind of human awareness.

Einstein's starting point was his 1905 paper, *The Electrodynamics of Moving Bodies*, in which he presented to the world the Special Theory of Relativity. The theory was developed in part to address situations within nature that do not conform to Newtons physical laws. In the paper, he articulated 2 basic fundamental principles. Firstly, that the speed of light is always the same and never changes, no matter who or what is observing it; 186,000 miles per second. This principle lies at the heart of the "big bang" theory of the origin of the universe, but that's another story. Einstein's second principle was that all observers moving at an unchanging speed, for instance on a planet Earth travelling through space at 67,000 mph, will naturally conform to the same physical laws. So far so good. However, using his favourite communication tool, mathematics, he was able to demonstrate that, logically, time itself must change according to the speed of a moving object relative to the position of someone observing it. This has been experimentally proven, demonstrating that an atomic clock ticks more slowly the faster it moves.

And that's not all. His later paper, *The Foundation of the General Theory of Relativity,* published in 1916, demonstrated the principle that the presence of matter, itself interchangeable with energy, causes space to curve. At a stroke, he had demolished the fundamental orthodoxy of over 250 years of Newtonian certainties. Where Newton had defined gravity as a force, obeying strict laws of physical motion, the new world of Einstein reinvented it as a curved area of space created by the presence of an object; a mass of some sort. In simple terms, we now know that time and space are not what we thought they were. The normal human perception of time is that its somehow a fixed point of reference, through which we navigate our life according to a strict timetable, moving from the past to the future. It never changes. It's us that has to constantly adjust to it; fighting it or surrendering to it, feeling that there's either too much of it or not enough. Similarly with space. It's somehow just there and we move about through it, from here to there. We change, it doesn't. Einstein demonstrated the exact opposite; that they, space & time, are not fixed and unchanging, rather mutating and shifting in some way relative to the way they're perceived. Conversely, perhaps Einstein was aligning science with a very simple reality that we've all known all along. As he pointed out: *"When you sit with a nice girl for two hours you think it's only a minute. But when you sit on a hot stove for a minute you think it's two hours. That's relativity."*

Einstein's dyslexic neurodiversity opened a can of worms there, but he wasn't finished yet. Again in 1905, not only did he publish proof that atoms actually exist, dispelling uncertainty about it, he also came up with a new theory of the nature of light. The prevailing orthodoxy since the time of Isaac Newton was that light is composed of waves of energy. If you think of sound, it is also waves of energy, transmitted through a medium, for instance air, before it hits your ear drums. That's why you can hear sound coming from your TV; soundwaves are being transmitted through the air in your front room. However, it can be demonstrated that sound can't pass through a vacuum. When it comes to light, we can clearly see the stars shining even though the light is passing through a vacuum. Throughout the 19th century, scientists sought to explain this conundrum with the

"Luminiferous Aether" theory, proposing that some undetectable invisible medium, aether, must be present throughout space in order to back up Newton's idea. They never did find it, but it wasn't for lack of trying.

Instead, Einstein created the quantum theory of light; that light is composed of tiny particles, quanta, of energy called photons. If he'd opened a can of worms with his theory of relativity, the birth of quantum physics threw a hand grenade into everything we thought was real. Before attempting to explain this, it's worth considering the words of quantum physicist John Wheeler (1911-2008): *"If you are not completely confused by quantum mechanics, you do not understand it."* Oh right... perhaps it's just me then? Well, no. According to Nobel prize winning physicist Richard Feynman (1918-1988): *"I think I can safely say that nobody understands quantum mechanics. The paradox is only a conflict between reality and your feeling of what reality ought to be"*. When the current UK government talks about wanting to increase the number of students studying science and mathematics, I'm not sure all this is quite what they had in mind!

The truth is that, in terms of the science, the new realities that quantum physics uncovers can only be described in mathematical terms... or so we are led to believe. The central concepts are 4-fold[28]. Firstly, that light, or

---

28. Information taken from Caltech: California Institute of Technology. <https://scienceexchange.caltech.edu/>

indeed anything else, can be shown to have the properties of particles OR waves of energy, depending on how they are observed or measured. This "wave-particle duality" has particular resonance when it comes to our human perception of stuff. We tend to think of objects, such as trees, cars, lumps of rock or whatever, as solid things; a conglomeration of particles. However, quantum science shows this to be not so. Instead, the appearance of these things is just that; an appearance of solidity, masking a reality of waves of energy. The second major concept of quantum physics, superposition, carries the idea one step forward. It's not so much that anything in the physical world can be either particles or waves. Rather, they can be both at the same time.

Not only that, but according to a 3rd concept, entanglement, an object or wave in one place and an object somewhere else, even a long way away, can actually be one and the same thing. Not merely that they can be connected together, but that are actually not separate. Well, whatever "stuff" may or may not be, at least we know it's there? Not quite, according to the final quantum concept: the uncertainty principle. Broadly speaking, anything in existence could be said to have both a position in space and a relative position in time; its speed of movement. The uncertainty principle is that if you can accurately measure one of these things, the other is uncertain. This has important philosophical implications, in that it suggests that anything of which we may be aware, with awareness as a key factor, may or may not be what we think; may or may not actually exist in an easily understandable way.

At this stage, it should be noted that the findings of quantum physics are mainly concerned with the nature and behaviour of very small objects; tiny sub-atomic particles or energetic events, beyond the range of ordinary human perception. However, those tiny things are the basic building blocks of everything that is, including us. The findings of quantum physics have completely destroyed the concept of the universe as a predictable mechanical machine operating according to simple laws, replacing it with something far less fixed, certain and comprehensible. The science has changed our perspective on everything, in particular replacing what can be observed "out there" with a heightened significance attached to the "in here"; the way that we observe and perceive things. The newer discipline of "quantum consciousness" takes the whole subject out of the realm of bespectacled mathematicians working in isolation in university physics departments to something of direct relevance to all of us; the nature & functioning of consciousness. It has long been known that human consciousness cannot be completely explained by neurone connections within the brain. Quantum consciousness is a set of theories that take certain quantum concepts such as entanglement and superposition to show how these, operating within the brain, try to explain aspects of consciousness and the workings of the human mind.

This area of science is very much in its infancy. One of the foundational facts of the study of quantum physics relates to the role of the observer; the way that what can be observed is not merely a detached objective occurrence, but rather varies according to the way that it is observed. The observer-scientist in the laboratory doesn't just look at a set of objective phenomena, but actually influences, or creates, what is observed by the simple act of observing it. The implications of this reality have been best explored by David Bohm (1917-1992). An associate of Albert Einstein, who called him his spiritual son, he was highly regarded as an outstanding scientist from an early age and wrote a standard textbook on quantum physics, *Quantum Theory*, published in 1951. Working closely with the acknowledged elites in the field of his time, he soon began to develop his own unique theories. However, two things happened to disrupt the early promise of his career progression. Firstly, he was accused of being a communist and hauled before the House Un-American Activities Committee; what we now call McCarthyism, after Senator Joseph McCarthy. Refusing to name any of his suspected communist associates resulted in him being arrested for contempt of Congress. Subsequently released without charge, he did however lose his job and was forced to move abroad, eventually ending up at Birkbeck College in London. The second thing that happened was that his new theories were not well received by his scientific peers. Met with outrage and hostility, even by Einstein, he was basically ostracised by the scientific community; a sad fate that befalls many original thinkers whose ideas conflict with the perceived orthodoxy of the day. It was only after his death in relative obscurity in London that the staggering implications of his theories began to receive the world changing attention that they truly deserve.

As a visionary quantum physicist in his own right, as well as a friend and scientific associate of Einstein, Bohm's starting point was a recognition that quantum physics and relativity were contradictory in some respects. He felt that both theories must point to a deeper theory that reconciled the two and which he called "quantum field theory". Expressed and understandable in mathematical language, he posited the existence of 2 orders of reality. Firstly the "explicate order" is that which we normally experience. Simply stated, most people experience themselves as a separate something called "me" which experiences things, events and processes occurring in the outer world, and that are not "me". These external events are encountered as apparently taking place within space, that stretches from near to far, and in time, that moves from the past to the future via the present. However, this level of experience, the normal human experience, proceeds from a different order of reality, the "implicate order", due to quantum processes taking place within the human brain. The implicate order is a domain of non-separateness, deriving from quantum science & relativity, in which time, space, mind, matter, me, not me, and energy are not different separate things, rather unified in a wholeness. Everything is One.

This of course is the realm of religion and spirituality. At a stroke, Bohm had managed to reconcile through science a basic division & contradiction that has been present throughout history; Science and Spirituality. This may partly explain why his ideas were so vehemently rejected by the scientific establishment in his day, but adopted after his death; at a time when our fragmented and increasingly dysfunctional world is in need of a new understanding that can bring us together. In his book, *Wholeness and the Implicate Order*, first published 1980, David articulates some of the implications of his discovery:

> *"The notion that the one who thinks (the Ego) is at least in principle completely separate from and independent of the reality that he thinks about is of course firmly embedded in our entire tradition... The notion that all these fragments are separately existent is evidently an illusion, and this illusion cannot do other than lead to endless conflict and confusion."*

"Endless conflict and confusion" could be an apt description of the current state of world society; suggesting that re-orienting ourselves to a modern scientific understanding of awareness might be a key catalyst for the transition into sustainability. A more recent 2004 quantum physics paper [29] sought to summarise all these issues into one overarching theory of consciousness; the core component of our experience, illusory or otherwise, of the world and ourselves. It summarised the 3 different theoretical approaches currently (2020) being undertaken by scientists. Firstly, that consciousness is the product of quantum processes taking place within the human brain. Secondly, that it doesn't really matter what happens within the brain. Rather, quantum processes themselves can explain consciousness. Finally, that consciousness and matter, stuff and mind, are two aspects of the same thing. They aren't separate things, rather one indivisible reality. As well as succinctly demonstrating how David Bohm's ideas have followed an historically well-trodden route from hostility & rejection to later acceptance, the theories derive in part from our old friends; the ancient Greeks. Thales (c. 624–545 BCE), observed that magnets and pieces of amber were able to move themselves. From this he deduced that they must have a mind. These ideas,

---

29. Atmanspacher, Harald, "Quantum Approaches to Consciousness", *The Stanford Encyclopedia of Philosophy* (Summer 2020 Edition), Edward N. Zalta (ed.), URL =
<https://plato.stanford.edu/archives/sum2020/entries/qt-consciousness/>.

ancient and modern, find a natural home in Pan-Psychism; the theory that everything in existence possesses, or is the expression of, consciousness. You may not be surprised to learn that, on googling the term, you'll find a considerable amount of outraged scoffing at the notion. Such is progress in the ongoing journey from illusion into truth. But if we were to learn that not only us, but trees, rocks, stars, the moon, fish, soil, water, etc., are not just dead things there for our own use & economic exploitation, but are conscious, how might that change things? Not only that, but that their consciousness is not separate from ours; one universal field of consciousness expressing itself through an infinite multiplicity of forms.

This chapter has had a very narrow scientific focus, looking exclusively at 20th century developments in the realm of subatomic physics. Findings in the field of quantum physics have basically uncovered a new understanding of reality, and especially hinted at a new sense of connection to the underlying unity of everything. Looked at on their own, unless one happens to be either a physicist... or a mystic... a response might be "So What?". There may well be, to use Bohm's terms, an implicate order behind the normal human perception of an explicate order; a realm of unity and non-separateness, which doesn't seem to directly interest most people. However, these discoveries in physics didn't happen in an isolated social vacuum and were not the only intellectual developments that took place within this historical period. The next chapter looks at other changes and insights in different fields of the human environment that have recently occurred, world changing in their own right, and that can be regarded as a 20th century "enlightenment". Just like the discoveries of David Bohm and many other scientific pioneers meet first with rejection and ridicule, then later acceptance, so the new thinking continues to meet scepticism in some quarters; from those who have a vested interest in maintaining an outdated order. Just as The Enlightenment that spanned the 17th and 18th centuries underpinned and made possible the transition of the Industrial Revolution, so the new thinking can be seen as inevitably heralding a brand-new transition, sooner or later, into a sustainable future as yet unknown.

Chapter 6

The 20th Century Enlightenment

"The upheaval of our world and the upheaval of our consciousness are one and the same". Carl Jung [30]

The previous chapter looked at the subject of quantum physics, showing how it has fundamentally altered our understanding of the nature of reality. Up to that point, "science" had been regarded as an objective discipline; the scientist in the laboratory objectively observing nature, creating hypotheses or theories to explain the way that nature worked and devising experiments to test the veracity of those theories. Quantum science changed the nature of science in two ways. Firstly, a greater emphasis on "thought experiments" expressed in mathematical terms, changing the way that scientists function, while secondly a new understanding that the scientist is not merely a passive observer of nature,

---

30. Carl Gustav Jung (2001). "Modern Man in Search of a Soul", p.215, Psychology Press

rather the act of observation changes what is seen. In other words, science had revealed the crucial importance of consciousness in our understanding of the world.

While this has revealed the role of consciousness in somewhat abstract terms, the nuts and bolts of consciousness, the way that it demonstrates in our day to day experience, became the province of the new domain of psychology, that massively grew throughout the 20th century. While proto-psychology can be seen in many ancient cultures, modern psychology relates most closely to the practice of psychiatry, developed during the 18th and 19th centuries. Throughout its development, and ever since, there has been debate as to whether it could be regarded as a true science. The issue is that, because we all operate from out of our own psychological processes, the question becomes one of whether true objectivity is possible. In effect, psychology has evolved into 2 distinct strands; on the one hand the study of what can be observed in human behaviour and on the other, a set of signposts or "map" for individual subjective exploration of our own psychological processes; thoughts, feelings and perceptions. Both strands concern themselves with a new subject study that has emerged over the last 100 years, namely what exactly does it mean to be a human being?

It was within this intellectual environment that emerged Sigmund Freud (1856-1939), the originator of psychoanalysis. Originally studying medicine and philosophy, Freud began his medical career in 1882 at the Vienna General Hospital. Time spent working in a psychiatric clinic and a local asylum, kickstarted his interest in this area of work. Believing that smoking helped him concentrate and produce better work, he is recorded as suggesting to a colleague that tobacco addiction was a substitute for masturbation, thereby at a stroke indicating both the direction of his future thinking and also saving his patients from potentially unnecessary trauma in their dealings with him!

Very much a product of the Victorian era, Freud was fascinated by the way that people seeking treatment for a whole range of psychological disorders often had in common deep and unresolved expressions of a primitive sexuality. He introduced into contemporary human thinking the idea of the "unconscious"; a part of ourselves that we are not aware of but is nonetheless influencing all our thinking, feeling, perception and experience. He introduced the concept of looking at the human psyche as made up of different parts or aspects. For instance, he termed the "super-ego" that part of us which is the product of upbringing, values, education, especially the urge to be a "good" person. In modern parlance, and as an example of how Freuds ideas have become embedded into the modern mind, we can call this "social conditioning". Often, especially in the Victorian age, this part was in conflict with what he termed the "id"; the part of ourselves that is primitive, instinctive and doesn't conform to our social conditioning. Most people, to different degrees will experience this conflict at some point and in some way. In Freuds system, the "ego", his third aspect, is the part of ourselves that balances id and super-ego. We usually conflate the ego with what we regard as the "self" – me.

Carl Jung (1875-1961) was initially a student of Freud and later broke away from him to establish a unique and innovative interpretation of the nature and function of the unconscious. He drew upon one of the ideas of Plato to pose the theory of "archetypes of the unconscious"; dynamic energy centers within the psyche that act as an underlying influence on imagination, fantasy, thought, perception and behaviour. He developed his theories through a long and intensive exercise of observing his own fantasies, creative imaginative processes and inner thought patterns. The archetypes have both a collective and an individual expression. Jung posited that the collective expression is embodied in the various myths and legends which are part of the culture of all civilizations, and which share certain characteristics in common. In all ages and places there are stories of brave heroes battling demons and dark entities, undertaking difficult ordeals and eventually winning the love of a beautiful maiden or a handsome prince. For Jung, these tales were not just entertaining stories, rather symbolic "maps" of the psychological processes which all individuals undergo in order to fulfil their inherent potential. He termed this inner personal journey "individuation"; the process of becoming a completely unique and free individual. This idea of human psychological growth and development has been a new key development of the 20th century.

A basic theme of this chapter is the way that the new ideas have not necessarily immediately led to a new way of living, a new transition, but instead have become co-opted into earlier patterns of thinking and behaving; creating conflict between the old and the new. Freuds and Jungs ideas might have, and for many people they still do, led to a completely different life orientation; one devoted to a deeper self-knowledge and understanding. However, in the case of Freud, his ideas are most closely represented in the modern world through the work of his nephew; Edward Bernays (1891-1995). Known as the "father of public relations", he focussed on Freuds insight that people are unconsciously driven by primitive instincts, to develop a comprehensive theory of marketing and propaganda as an appeal to those instincts. He worked very closely with both governments and large corporations and his ideas are now very much an integral part of the political and economic establishments, as they seek to persuade the people to adopt their agendas, subscribe to their ideas and buy stuff they don't really need. An example of his principles to people of my generation was the way that motor cars were usually advertised throughout the late 1950s and 60s with a picture of the shiny new vehicle surrounded by nubile bikini clad young women. The clear message to the male heterosexual unconscious was "buy this car and you'll get laid". The message may or may not have worked, but car ownership substantially increased. More latterly in the modern day, marketing is directed to the urge for freedom; branded as the freedom to buy products that enhance your unique individual potential, thereby using Carl Jung's ideas.

An early success of Bernays' principles was a 1929 campaign to introduce cigarette addiction to women. Aware of the growth of feminism in the early years of the century, his work led to cigarettes being advertised as "feminist torches of freedom". It may not have done much for feminism, but it certainly increased the profits of the tobacco companies. The 20th century rise of feminism began with the era of the suffragettes. Ever since the democratic experiments of the early Greeks, representative governance, along with much else, had been the exclusive preserve of just an arbitrary half of humanity; men. In 1903, Emmeline Pankhurst and her daughters decided that enough was enough and founded the Women's Social and Political Union (WSPU) in Manchester. Moving to London in 1906 brought them closer to the seat of government and their aim: votes for women. The movement very rapidly grew, both in the numbers of followers and in the level of conflict it provoked with those who didn't want to change; principally the government.

In many ways their campaign techniques set a precedent for modern day protest movements, most notably those of Extinction Rebellion and Just Stop Oil. June 1908 saw a mass demonstration of 300,000 march to Hyde Park, showing participants dressed in their distinctive purple, white and green colours. By 1909, the weekly newspaper, "Votes for Women" had a circulation of 22,000, distributed through 90 WSPU branches throughout the country. A 1914 direct action saw one Mary Richardson enter the National Gallery and slash a valuable painting of the nude Venus. At her trial, she spoke in her defence: "*I have tried to destroy the picture of the most beautiful woman in mythological history as a protest against the Government for destroying Mrs. Pankhurst who is the most beautiful character in modern history*". The suffragettes also disrupted the free movement of traffic, in a further echo of modern-day protests.[31]

Over a thousand suffragettes were imprisoned for their actions. Many claimed to be political prisoners; a claim that was refuted, leading to hunger strikes and a government led policy of forced feeding. While the outbreak of the first world war in 1914 brought an end to

---

31. Information taken from Museum of London: Who Were the Suffragettes?. <https://www.museumoflondon.org.uk/>

the campaign and the release of all prisoners, 1918 saw the granting by the House of Lords of a limited vote to just some women over the age of 30. It took another 10 years for a new law to be passed giving the vote to all women over the age of 21; the same as men. The genie of women's liberation had been let out of the bottle; a movement that had been gestating for a long time. The origins of the movement began with the 18th century enlightenment and the rare, because female, figure of Mary Wollstonecraft (1759-1797). In her 1792 book, *A Vindication of the Rights of Woman*[32], she argued that women are not naturally inferior to men, instead equally gifted human beings deserving of the same human rights. For Mary, the key issue that produced this historical misconception was lack of education; a struggle that continues to this day in various guises, not least the need for men to be educated as to a just & harmonious relationship with women.

Amongst the beneficiaries of the new era of female emancipation and educational opportunities, Rachel Carson (1907-1964) has cemented a significant place in 20th century history. Born to a farming family in Pennsylvania, her childhood was spent exploring the countryside around the farm and writing stories about animals; having her first published story in print at the

---

32. Wollstonecraft, Mary, 1759-1797. A Vindication of the Rights of Woman: with Strictures on Political and Moral Subjects. London :Printed for J. Johnson, 1792.

age of 10. A love of the natural world featured heavily in all her work. Especially, a fascination with the sea prompted her to study biology at university level, before entering a career as a marine biologist. However, she also continued her writing and had many pieces published in a wide variety of magazines, as well as script writing for radio and films. An overall theme of all her writing was to provoke a love and respect for the natural world; winning many awards and two honorary doctorates.

In 1945, Rachel had first encountered, through her work as a biologist, a new pesticide which was entering the market; DDT. The chemical was initially lauded as a very effective means of killing unwanted pests, but also raised significant concerns over its harmful effects on the environment and other life forms. For Rachel Carson, this prompted her for more detailed work on the effects of the use of synthetic chemicals in agriculture, leading to the 1962 publication of the book for which she is best known; *Silent Spring* [33]. The title was prompted by a letter from a friend, disclosing how the aerial spraying of DDT to kill mosquitos was also killing the birds in her neighbourhood. By this time, Rachel had become a very skilled writer, combining scientific facts with a provocative & resonant poetic appeal to the emotions. The book had a potent dual effect. Widely credited with starting the environmental protection movement,

---

33. Carson, R.L., 2002. *Silent Spring*, London: Penguin.

continuing to this day, much support from the scientific establishment caused it to become a major influence on the development of the social movements of the 1960s. However, it also prompted an extreme backlash from the pharmaceutical industry, continuing to this day, over a range of products and practices. Much of the rest of Rachel's life was spent battling the industry; exposing widespread misinformation, propaganda, dirty tricks and corruption; all in the name of preserving their profits at whatever cost. Renowned naturalist David Attenborough has cited *Silent Spring* as the second most influential scientific publication of all time, after Charles Darwin's "The Origin of Species". DDT was only finally banned worldwide in 2001.

> *"The more clearly we can focus our attention on the wonders and realities of the universe about us, the less taste we shall have for destruction."* Rachel Carson.

For Rachel Carson, and many others, her work highlighted a basic conflict between the needs or demands of economic growth & profitability on the one hand and the needs of humans and the natural world on the other; a basic division running throughout history. This conflict was best highlighted and analysed in the work of a German born philosopher, economist and political theorist who holds the dubious distinction of being one of the most divisive figures in history; a man revered as a wise saviour by some and the embodiment of cosmic evil by others. Karl Marx (1818-1883) produced his written works in the 19th century, but it is throughout the 20th century, continuing up to the modern day, that his influence has had the greatest impact. His basic idea is that, throughout history, human societies have evolved through a tension & conflict between two "classes" of people; a ruling class who govern the economic system and a working class who depend on the economic system to maintain their living. He called this economic system "capitalism" and argued that the inherent tensions and conflicts within it would inevitably lead to a new form of society, called socialism or communism, in which the human alienation and destructive impulses caused by capitalism would be no more. His voluminous works are not easy to read and have themselves spawned a multitude of offshoots, hybrids and variations; both vehemently for and equally against Marxism.

The main effects of Marx and Marxism within the 20th century have been two-fold. Firstly, his ideas are universally studied within higher education and beyond, mainly in an endeavour to formulate an understanding of what precisely socialism is or could be; an antidote to the sickness of the modern world. His writings have become the groundwork of the new discipline of sociology; which seeks to reveal the hidden factors underpinning the social world. For every understanding in this field, and measures intended to create greater social justice, there has been an equal backlash from some quarters, to the position where the very mention of his name is associated with extreme hostility and opprobrium. The whole subject of generic Marxism and socialism has become one of the leading battlegrounds of intellectual warfare in the world today. The second area where Marxism has had a potent influence is the field of political revolutions. Beginning notably with the 1917 Russian revolution and the 1949 Chinese communist revolution, there have been no fewer than 45 political revolutions throughout the world, inspired by Marxist ideals. Many of these locations are still immersed in conflict; both internally and in external tensions with other nations and groups. Committed Marxists might argue that this is because revolutionary socialist ideals have not been properly implemented. Others might argue that perhaps the reason lies in a misunderstanding of what socialism actually is; a political/economic system or a state of consciousness. Wherever the truth lies, the old dictum of "not talking about politics or religion if you want to maintain friendly relationships" might certainly hold.

Psychology & psychotherapy, environmentalism and socialism were all elements contributing to the western youth movement of the 1960s. However, one element was still missing; spirituality. Up until the 20th century, religion and spirituality in the west were mainly dominated by the 3 "religions of the book"; Christianity,

Judaism and Islam. All take their guidance from a book, all hold to a general belief that their way is the correct way and the others wrong, and all hold to a doctrine of a great leader who will emerge to guide humanity out of the current era of darkness and confusion into a promised new age. For Judaism, this is the long-awaited appearance of the Messiah. For Islam it is the Imam Mahdi and for Christianity it is the reappearance of Christ. For most people, one's religion, or lack of it, is mainly down to the culture in which one happens to be born, combined with the unique times in which we happen to live. The "times in which we live", from a spiritual perspective, could be said to have been very much influenced in the late 19th century with the ideas of one man in particular, whose legacy has grown throughout the 20th century and up to the modern day.

Representing India at the 1893 "Parliament Of The World´s Religions" in Chicago USA, Swami (meaning "knower & master of oneself") Vivekenanda introduced to the western world the teachings of Vedanta (knowledge, liberation) and Yoga (union). A gifted orator with a striking exotic appearance, his presentations at the parliament made him the undoubted star of the occasion and led to hundreds of talks and lectures across America over the next few years; extensively and glowingly reported in the media. While coming from a Hindu background, his earlier life had been devoted to discovering a new role for Indian spirituality in the modern world. A deep intellectual with a gift for speed reading and photographic memory recall, his studies covered the areas of religion, history, art, social science, literature and philosophy; an echo of the scholars of the 18th century European enlightenment. Interested in religion from an early age, his studies of western movements caused him to reject many of the dogmas and beliefs of Hinduism, as well as vocally advocate for the equal rights of women. Contact with an American religious movement, transcendentalism, especially influenced him, with its emphasis on direct personal religious experience in preference to reasoning and theology.

While the "religions of the book" ascribe divinity to just one figure, the founder of the religion, within the Vedantic understanding anyone can realise divinity; referring to a natural state that has become lost or obscured to us. For Vivekananda, the ultimate expression was Advaita Vedanta; also known as non-duality. Expressed simply, this school of thought posits that the normal human experience of being a separate self, or "me" is itself an illusion; which once realised opens up entry for the person into a divine "heavenly" state. Coinciding with the decline in orthodox religions throughout the 20th century, Vedanta, along with other so-called Eastern expressions of spirituality such as Buddhism, Zen, Taoism, have struck a vital chord within people. Of particular note, the teachings of Vedanta coincide exactly with the scientific quantum theories of David Bohm; discussed in the previous chapter and reconciling a centuries old division between Religion and Science.

Along with the new discoveries and insights taking place in the early 1900s, there was also taking place a transition in the realms of Art and Music. While art had for centuries been concerned with the use of colour, form, tone, line and texture to depict people, nature and landscapes in a variety of settings, real or imaginary, the early 1900s saw a radical departure into abstraction, devoid of recognisable subject matter beyond the raw feelings of the artist. Similarly in music, the melting pot of cultures present within the USA, especially the legacy of transported slaves, gave rise to the new music of Jazz. Wild, passionate, improvised and fun, the 1920s and 1930s are now known as the jazz age. As with all new innovations, the new music stirred up fears within the establishment, warning of a catastrophic descent into primitive emotions, violence, lawlessness and rampant sexuality; fears no doubt partly influenced by the jazz musicians' drug of choice - marijuana.

However, by the outbreak of World War 2, the latest incarnation of jazz, the swing bands, had become firmly embedded in the American cultural consciousness, serving as a beacon of hope and freedom through the difficulties of the war years and the fight against extreme right-wing fascist ideology. The end of the long war years introduced a breathing space into the American and European psyche and provided a fertile environment for a brand new cultural phenomenon; the rise of youth culture. In the late 1940s and early 1950s a new musical form began to grow out of jazz, blues, gospel church music and country music. Essentially employing a dance rhythm, accentuated by a back beat played on a snare drum, a Cleveland, Ohio, disc jockey called Alan Freed began playing this music on his radio programmes in 1951; a music he called "rock n' roll". The fact that Alan Freed reportedly believed the name to be a synonym for sexual intercourse, combined with the widespread horror and panic that this provoked amongst parents, ensured that the new music became enthusiastically adopted almost exclusively by young people. The 1960s were not far away now.

A number of influences, including rock n' roll and a new form of socially aware folk music, shaped the development of youth culture over the next few years. A Swiss chemist, Albert Hoffman (1906-2008), was engaged in the work of creating new analeptics; medicines that stimulate the central nervous system and are used in the treatment of a range of disorders, including depression and attention deficit hyperactive disorders. Their main use is as an anaesthetic recovery tool. Albert had been looking at substances derived from ergot; a fungus that infects grain. The main substance found, lysergic acid, could be further refined into different chemicals and he had made 24 different derivatives of it; so far unusable for the purposes he had intended. His 25th attempt in 1938 produced a breakthrough, but not of a nature he expected. Called LSD 25, he inadvertently ingested a microscopic amount through his skin and reported on its effects: "Kaleidoscopic, fantastic images surged in on me, alternating, variegated, opening and then closing themselves in circles and spirals, exploding in coloured fountains, rearranging and hybridizing themselves in constant flux. It was particularly remarkable how every acoustic perception, such as the sound of a door handle or a passing automobile, became transformed into optical perceptions. Every sound generated a vividly changing image, with its own consistent form and colour."[34]

The world's first LSD or acid "trip" provoked very considerable interest in both the psychiatric and military establishments. The drug company Sandoz licensed it for distribution to researchers, in an attempt to find a marketable use for it. LSD assisted psychotherapy was widely practiced throughout the 1950s and early 1960s, showing particular value in the treatment of alcoholism. At first it was believed to mimic schizophrenia, until research showed that it could induce transcendental experiences of a vastly enhanced consciousness, with a

---

34. From Rolling Stone magazine, APRIL 19, 2018: "Flashback: LSD Creator Albert Hofmann Drops Acid for the First Time".

permanent benefit to the individual, most closely resembling classic accounts of mystical experience. This led to LSD being termed a "psychedelic" drug; literally meaning *mind manifesting*. At the same time, the military began experimenting with its use as an enhanced interrogation tool, due to its capacity to reduce potential enemy combatants into fits of giggles, unable to any longer take seriously their prior commitment to violence and warfare. However, the main "use" of LSD became as a drug of choice to vast numbers of young people in the youth-led counter-culture of the 1960s. The view of the US government rapidly became that it was a threat to national values, especially destroying support for the now widely discredited Vietnam war effort, prompting it to being made illegal in 1968. However, that didn't stop its use. It should be noted, that in addition to leading to genuine spiritual journeys of self-discovery for many, there were also less frequent instances of severe psychological breakdown and permanent psychosis. LSD is potentially very dangerous stuff and not to be casually tampered with.

For many, their experiments with LSD naturally led to an involvement with what became known as the "human potential" movement. The term was coined by writer Aldous Huxley (1894-1963), author of numerous books, including *Brave New World* (1932) and notably *The Doors of Perception* (1954), being an account of his experiments with mescalin; an LSD related naturally occurring compound. Founded in 1962, the Esalen Institute, located on the Californian coastline and leading source of the movement, sought to explore non drug-based techniques for expanding human consciousness; the human potential. Pioneering many beliefs and practices that have now become part of the mainstream, their work covered such areas as alternative medicine, eastern philosophies, meditation, mindfulness, renewable energy, yoga, massage, organic food, ecology and psychotherapy. An early group leader there, Carl Rogers (1902-1987) founded the modern widespread practice of Counselling, while a multitude of different psychotherapies find their contemporary expression in Cognitive Behaviour Therapy. While nowadays counselling and psychotherapy are regarded as a treatment for mental & emotional traumas & disorders, at the time of their creation they were seen as tools for anyone who wished to become a better functioning human being.

The decade of the 1960s marked a potential turning point in human affairs as a new group emerged into US and European awareness. The average high street, basking in the affluent & euphoric after-glow of the "never had it so good" 1950s [35], began to see weird and wonderful people making their appearance, like an invasion of some alien latter day gothic tribe. Dressed in colourful

---

35. "You've never had it so good". Quote from a speech by UK prime minister Harold Macmillan in July 1957.

exotic clothing, the boys with long hair and beards, often surrounded by the now familiar aroma of marijuana and patchouli oil, the hippies made their public debut, rock and roll became progressive, London started swinging and the dawning of the age of aquarius was announced. To define the beliefs of the 1960s in terms of flared trousers, communes and unrealistic pipe dreams is to miss an important point. These people were mainly educated, cultured, philosophical and possessed of a pronounced goodwill. Peace and Love was their motto and they appeared at a time when peace and love were sorely needed.

October 1962 saw the Cuban missile crisis and the world coming very close indeed to the long-anticipated nuclear war between Russia and America. Taking place over several days, and largely involving the participation of just 2 individuals, the Russian leader Khrushchev and US president Kennedy, a desperate game of brinkmanship, bluff and double bluff was played out in the full glare of the worlds media, while the people waited, held their breath and united in prayer. Appearing on prime time television, Kennedy announced to the world: "It shall be the policy of this nation to regard any nuclear missile launched from Cuba against any nation in the Western Hemisphere as an attack by the Soviet Union on the United States, requiring a full retaliatory response upon the Soviet Union." Fortunately, the leaders stepped back at the last moment, MAD (mutually assured destruction) was avoided for the time being and we got back to business as usual; with the added addition that John Fitzgerald Kennedy had now cemented his place within history as the great white hope for a better world. That is until November 1963, when a confident Kennedy, out campaigning for a re-election most felt he would win, happened to be assassinated in Dealey Plaza, Dallas, Texas. Bringing a new term into world grammar, "conspiracy theory", the facts around the event have still never been properly resolved. The main outcome has been to bring into focus a new awareness, initially to the burgeoning hippy counter-culture, from whence it has spread throughout the world into the modern age: your government is lying to you.

While all this was yet to potentially emerge into the awareness of a young Worthing resident, Richard Grave, April 1961 found him taking advantage of a different kind of 1960s innovation bursting onto the scene. DIY (do it yourself) was becoming all the rage; a harbinger of doom to painters and decorators everywhere, but signifying new horizons of creativity and money saving for the rest of us. Wrestling with the problem of what grade of sandpaper was needed for the necessary preparation for a bit of painting in his new rented home, his musings were very profoundly interrupted when a "bearded Christlike figure" suddenly appeared to him; the first of many such apparitions informing Grave of the imminent reappearance of Christ due to humanities dire condition. The story was picked up in the May 1961 edition of "Psychic News", and it rapidly became clear that it was not only Grave with whom the presence had communicated. Rather, a being identifying itself as "limitless love and truth" was simultaneously communicating telepathically with many worldwide, leading to the formation of a global network of groups under the umbrella label of the Universal Link Revelation. To Grave, the being gave the following message: "No one can know the day nor the hour of my coming, or when the great Universal Revelation will be enacted; however by Christmas morning 1967, I will have revealed myself through the medium of nuclear evolution. This is my Plan which is absolute." [36]

Within the Universal Link network, this was widely interpreted to mean that the world would come to the brink of nuclear war, which it soon did, and at the moment that the button was pressed, rather than the planet and all of us disintegrating into a lethal fireball, the universal link revelation would occur and many people would find themselves experiencing a state of "higher consciousness"; a realisation of the mind-based illusory nature of the separate self. The general consensus was that rather than the messiah appearing as a single individual to lead humanity into the promised

---

36. Source: Jon R Stone, 2013, *Expecting Armegeddon: Essential Readings in Failed Prophecy*, Routledge.

new age of aquarius, it would be a whole group of people performing that function.

While we clearly survived 1967, it was indeed a momentous year; the world´s first heart transplant, mass availability of colour TVs, the first major oil pollution incident as the Torrey Canyon ran aground at Lands End, first recorded use of the term "personal computer" by Hewlett-Packard, the 6 day war in the middle east... and Elvis Presley marrying Priscilla, thereby breaking the hearts of millions of young women worldwide. The year also saw arguably the single instance that best symbolised and defined both the obstacles and opportunities marking our transition into a planetary post-industrial digital age. Utilising the new satellite technology, the very first live global television link in 1967 was a programme called "Our World". Co-ordinated by the European Broadcasting Union as a collaboration between 14 countries, the British section came from London; beamed to a further 26 countries and watched by 350 million people. The programme brief was to come up with a song containing a simple message that would be understood by all nationalities. A globally revered ambassador for peace and defining himself as a revolutionary artist whose art is dedicated to change, John Lennon came up with:

> *"There´s nothing you can know that isn´t known*
> *Nothing you can see that isn´t shown*

*Nowhere you can be that isn´t where you´re meant to be
It´s easy... All you need is love"*

While this event, and indeed the song, clearly has immense symbolic significance, there was another occasion that perhaps puts a more contemporary meaningful interpretation to the Universal Link and a post-Armageddon global society. Described as the first "human be-In", the Gathering of The Tribes was a January 1967 event in Golden Gate Park, San Francisco. Widely understood to be the definitive event that forever memorialised 1967 as the "summer of love", the tribes that gathered were essentially three in number; three interlinked strands of culture that are of immense significance to the crises and challenges that we face today. Firstly, a back-to-nature movement had seen more than a million young Americans, mainly young, middle class and college-educated, leave their homes in the suburbs and cities to seek a life more in tune with the natural world; growing their own food, generating sustainable energy and living a simpler lifestyle closer to the Earth, in harmonious co-existence with other life forms. Secondly, the "truth seekers" were those who derived meaning from the rapid influx of Eastern spiritual practices, combined with the developments in psychotherapy that occurred during this decade. Thirdly, a coalition of student political movements for social justice, the "new left", focussed on issues such as the anti-war movement, a rebellion against capitalist excess, women´s liberation, human rights and new models of participative democracy, amongst others.

The fusion and widespread adoption of these three strands... all of them... perhaps precisely represents the blueprint that can carry us through the Armageddon scenario that we now face and into a new transition. However, almost immediately, the hippie dream soured and became ridiculed in public awareness. Substance gave way to Style in the 1970s and politics took a hard turn to the right. The peaceful benevolent influence of psychedelia turned into a more sinister emphasis on hard drugs and benign ideas of a liberal socio-political radicalism gave way to the values of the market and the pre-eminence of the bottom line. Currently, it is becoming ever more visible that there is a global endeavour by dark forces to attempt to create a new dictatorial world order characterised by climate change denial, unrestrained profit-led abuse of the natural world, dismantling of peaceful co-operative alliances between nations, loss of civil liberties & control over personal data, withdrawal from human rights conventions, fostering of hostility between peoples, fake news, undermining of democracy, disregard for the law and suppression of a free press.

The optimistic certainties of the 1960s have been cast aside and given way to progressively deepening crisis.

Chapter 7

Mother Earth: Jewel of the Cosmos

We have never been more affluent or had more opportunities to purchase luxuries our forebears could only dream about, enjoying unprecedented leisure time. We can travel with ease to wherever we want to go; or at least we used to. Our TV, Smartphone and PC give us access to instant awareness of a global culture, arts and literature formally the preserve of a privileged few. Fresh water, wholesome food and modern healthcare are instantly available to most, although difficulties with these are beginning to appear. It all sounds so good. And yet, apart from those who are literally going mad in the midst of this materialistic utopia, many more experience a general sense of unease and discomfort. Nothing you can necessarily put your finger on, just a feeling that somehow something is not quite right.

Maybe it's the awareness that while many are becoming wealthier, actually levels of extreme global poverty are increasing, with vast numbers dying unnecessary and avoidable deaths for the lack of a few pence. Or maybe, as we sit in the daily traffic jam belching out poisonous fumes into the atmosphere, there is that uncomfortable thought that it's actually us who are creating a global environmental catastrophe. "Oh well.. can't be helped.. I have to pay the mortgage, the gas bill, the life insurance, the council tax, the loan repayment. These problems are the job of government to solve... Just as long as my own taxes don't go up, everything will be alright." Or maybe, it's something about the way that things are changing at work in a way that compromises my values, but if I speak out they won't like it.. so best to keep quiet for the sake of the pension, the holidays and a quiet life.

The point is that rather than appreciating our relative stupendous wealth, many actually feel poorer. We have, bit by bit, moved into a society where the constant message inflicted on us by advertisers is that, to be happy, we need MORE. More stuff, more drink, more sex, more food, more holidays, more distractions and of course that supposed panacea for all ills; more money. And when we are still not happy, we need more people to blame; the government, young people, benefit claimants, the wealthy, the opposite sex, migrants, the EU…

What is actually going on here? An imaginary visitor from another planet might be forgiven for thinking that they had inadvertently strayed into the galactic lunatic asylum, rather than a "jewel of the cosmos", managed by a human species that possesses the imagination, intelligence and technological ability to solve any problem with which it is confronted, but instead appears to be locked onto a trajectory of global catastrophe. A simple answer is that the problem is human nature and nothing can be done about it. A slightly more complex answer is that the political, media and financial establishments have tied us into a lifestyle that promises us everything but instead delivers a subtle imprisonment that is difficult to escape from, while the cell walls progressively close in. Also, it indicates that the needed change is somehow achieved out there, with more rules, more procedures, more e-mails, initiatives and money, rather than in here, the only place where true lasting change can occur.

Globally, we are in a state of crisis. We are used to hearing the word in a number of situations, for example the "environmental & climate crisis" or the "crisis in the economy", the small boats crisis, the cost of living crisis or even an "identity crisis". Individuals use the word to describe difficult circumstances that appear problematical, either to themselves or others. Once a solution to the problem is found and acted on, or otherwise resolved, then the crisis is said to have dissipated. But what exactly is a crisis and what makes it different from the regular sort of challenge that has always been part of everyday life?

We normally operate psychologically and emotionally in a constant endeavour to maintain balance and a sense of well-being; automatically adjusting our thoughts and feelings to the moment-by-moment changes encountered in life. Something happens, we think and feel, which in turn prompts action intended to lead to a sense of pleasure. If it leads to discomfort, then we try something else. When functioning normally, this process carries on relatively effortlessly and largely unconsciously. The nature of the thinking and feeling tends to be spontaneous and automatic. Sure, we encounter difficulties and challenges, but nothing that we can´t deal with. Our patterns of emotional and psychological response, created by experience, habit and knowledge, are enough to carry us on. They serve to keep us more or less in a state of harmony, while working to minimise any sense of conflict. However, when a true "crisis" arises, this process breaks down. The habitual thoughts and feelings we generate no longer serve to bring us to that point. Tension and discomfort become magnified and move out of our control. The normal psychological processes no longer work to restore that sense of balance and well-being. This is where we are collectively now, although many would deny it.

Such a situation of escalating imbalance could not occur within nature. It is a peculiarly human characteristic, indicating just how disconnected & alienated we have become from our natural state. Named after the Greek goddess who personifies the living earth, the Gaia hypothesis was developed in the 1970s by English scientist and futurist James Lovelock (1919-2022) working in partnership with US microbiologist Lynn Margulis (1938-2011); mentioned in chapter 3 for her work on the evolution of co-operation and altruism. The hypothesis states that the entire planet; living things, the environment and the atmosphere, constitute a single, unified, self-regulating entity. The entire system continuously adjusts itself and all inter-species relationships to ensure the maintenance of optimal conditions for the well-being of all life. Within this context, the climate and environmental crisis is not necessarily a problem. Nature is naturally adjusting and responding. Rather, it is us, the human community, that is out of step. Be in no doubt: for nature, for Gaia, life will probably carry on. However, whether or not humans can survive in the ensuing future world depends on us, specifically whether or not we are willing and able to adjust our civilisation and culture to bring it back into harmony with nature; to create an ecological civilisation.

Ecology is the study of how organisms relate to and interact with other organisms and their environment, in order to maximise the health and well-being of all. It is the study of relationships. The network of relationships is termed an "ecosystem". Within a functioning ecosystem, natural processes take place that have their sole purpose the health and well-being of all components of that system. For millions of years the natural world has evolved to produce an astounding and utterly beautiful array of countless organisms, providing us with nourishing food, fresh air, clean water and medicines. Most importantly, nature and our contact with it makes us feel good. The destruction and abuse of nature makes us feel bad. The original human inhabitants of the Earth, indigenous peoples, have always recognised this and have lived a life that honours and respects underlying ecological principles. It can be argued that it is only with the advent of the industrial age, with its emphasis on the pre-eminent value of economic growth at all costs, that we have embarked on a process that seems intent on destroying the very thing that supports us to live.

Austrian born physicist and systems theorist Fritjof Capra[37] (born 1939) is a leading voice for the building of sustainable human communities based around an understanding of ecological principles in nature. Capra has identified 6 basic principles, beginning with "Networks". Within nature, all members of an ecological community are interconnected in a "web of life"; dependent for their health on co-operation within

---

[37]. A Vienna-born physicist and systems theorist, Capra first became popularly known for his book, *The Tao of Physics*, which explored the ways in which modern physics was changing our worldview from a mechanistic to a holistic and ecological one. <https://www.fritjofcapra.net/>

and between species and their environment. And yet, in the human sphere, we are constantly told that the secret to happiness and economic well-being lies in becoming more competitive. Within an ecological civilisation, co-operation, rather than competition, between people, and with nature, is a defining feature. Conventional economics ignores interaction with the environment; making profit & economic growth more valuable than the health of the environment, the air, the soil and the water. In an ecological civilisation, the health of the natural ecosystem, which nourishes and sustains us all, becomes the guiding principle of economic activity.

Capra's second principle of "Nested Systems" identifies the way that throughout nature we find multi-levelled structures of smaller systems nesting within larger systems; maintaining their own integrity while also being part of a larger whole. In human terms, the local community is an ecosystem within larger structures; the city, region, nation, continent, global community. However, decisions affecting that community are most often directed at the national or global level. The new political philosophy of Localism supports local production and consumption of goods, local control of government, and promotion of local history, local culture and local identity. It also supports more deliberative democracy; by which local residents are empowered to more effectively engage with and contribute to local decision making. These innovations, in a locally agreed form, combined with an internationally agreed common standard of values, are one basis of a new ecological civilisation. The United Nations Declaration Of Universal Human Rights, adopted in 1948, is one already agreed common standard.

The principle of "Cycles" concerns the way that energy and resources are constantly cycled throughout the nested ecosystems. Within nature, nothing is wasted. Everything that dies becomes food for something else. In autumn, the leaves fall from the trees and are broken down by worms and bacteria into their constituent parts. This then provides nutrients for the next season of growth. Compare this to our current human civilisation where the waste products of our industrial processes & lifestyle serve not to support further life but to destroy it. Almost everyone recognises that this is wrong. An ecological civilisation puts an immediate halt to destructive & harmful pollution and waste; in recognition that it is seriously damaging both us and the natural world.

The fourth principle of "Flows" enhances the need for a continual flow of energy and resources to maintain the health of the system. At the very heart of this situation, it is the constant flow of solar energy from the sun that drives all of nature. Latest research[38] indicates that more than 99.9% of peer-reviewed scientific papers agree that climate change is mainly caused by humans, according to a survey of 88,125 climate related studies. To be specific, the human agency is a triple process of obtaining our energy from fossil fuel sources, widespread deforestation which removes the natural solar driven conversion of carbon dioxide back into oxygen and a growing technological culture which is increasingly energy dependent. The new ecological civilisation will see an end to energy generation from fossil fuels, combined with a rapid re-forestation and an emphasis on energy efficiency.

Life at the individual level and evolution at the species level depend on a continuous process of "Development", creativity and mutual adaptation. In the human realm, the current education system was designed to create a population suitable for the industrial era, now coming to its end. In an ecological civilisation the aim of education is to develop an integrated and unique person; someone at ease with themselves, aware of their true relationship with the cosmos, in which individual interests & aptitudes are nurtured and developed. Health, happiness and well-being is the paramount aim, rather than simply the production of obedient cogs in an economic machine.

---

38. Mark Lynas *et al*, 2021, Greater than 99% consensus on human caused climate change in the peer-reviewed scientific literature, *Environmental Research Letters,* **16** 114005, 19 October 2021

Finally, in keeping with the principles of the Gaia hypothesis, natural processes always move towards a state of "Dynamic Balance". As human beings, we are an integral part of the global ecosystem; not just our physical presence, but also our culture, behaviour and ways of thinking. Two things are happening in the world today. Firstly, a widespread "awakening" is taking place to the depth of the mess that we find ourselves in. In ecological terms, we are completely out of step with the functioning of natural planetary ecosystems. Secondly, we are confronted with an enormous resistance to change. Virtually every aspect of our culture and civilisation has become locked into a completely unnatural mode of being, such that the transition to an ecological civilisation will demand a total re-orientation of the human presence within the earth community; a transformation of all our institutions. However, we´ve been here before. The 18th century Industrial Revolution was also an enormous transition, that began in small ways, gaining momentum over the ensuing years. The difference now is that whereas the Industrial Revolution was driven by a small number of people, vast multitudes are now heeding the call from nature.

In every corner of the planet, people everywhere recognise the need for these types of change. For a very large proportion of these people, the intelligent people of goodwill, the main thrust of their thinking and in many cases their actions, revolve around an effort to persuade, lobby for and demand that the political and economic establishment changes. A multitude of petitions, conferences, outraged social media posts, letters to MPs and well-meaning small groups maintain the pressure and, barring the odd minor success, nothing appears to change; beyond the occasional false dawn being followed by a deepened sense of disillusionment and despair. In fact, the problems are getting progressively worse. The difficulty can be summarised as clearly stating that the establishment can't and won't change. Our leaders are not demonstrating effective leadership, scientists warn that climate change irreversible tipping points may now have been breached, trees are still being unnecessarily chopped down and the insanity of warfare is visible for all to see. All these and many more issues are actually perceived as quite logical, indeed necessary, to the systems and organisations promoting them. Trillions of dollars and a vast web of financial relationships affecting almost everybody are at stake. The forces that have a vested interest in things not changing are immense and apparently much more powerful than the well-meaning individual or small group dedicated to benevolent change. Not only the systems themselves, but also the traditional ways of trying to influence & modify those systems are ineffective to deal with the global crisis in which we are immersed.

It can begin to look very much like we, as a species, are

doomed. However, the purpose of this book has been to show the way that transitional periods, signifying profound and long-lasting change, have been a key feature of the ongoing historical process of social evolution of the human presence on planet earth. Not only that, but since the advent of the 20th century the building blocks or core principles & ideas of a new type of global society have been slowly taking shape. None of the previous transitions have been initiated by an apparent crisis, which is what makes the need for this one so different. On a personal level a crisis can be experienced as valuable, if it turns our attention inwards to an understanding that it´s our self rather than the world outside that needs to change. This is not a sign of failure, rather possibly one of the most empowering experiences anyone can have. At some point, nature dictates that a caterpillar will turn into a butterfly. For the caterpillar, survival depends on keeping a low profile, crawling, hiding under leaves, anything to avoid being seen and eaten by birds. This is what it knows and is certain of. It´s what being a caterpillar is all about. Within the experience of caterpillars, it´s termed "normal". Everything about being a butterfly is wrong for the caterpillar: the irresistible urge to spread wings, to leave the security of earth and fly joyously through the air, to become drunk on the nectar of flowers and to be universally admired as a creature of great beauty. The caterpillar can be said to be in a state of acute crisis... until it realises that it is now a butterfly.

In a similar way, just as the transition of the industrial revolution, leading to the conditions of the modern world, was based on a few simple ideas, so the enlightenment of the 20th century points the way to the characteristics of the new transition taking place. The caterpillar has already turned into a butterfly, but is not yet fully aware of it. What do we now know that evidences this? We know that the multiple crises of the modern world have their cause in a political/economic system that regards economic growth & profitability as more important than human, natural & community well-being. Because of the way that the money system works, new money created by debt, it compels us into the necessity for endless economic growth… and that this is destructive and unsustainable. We know that the solution to this is system change, while also knowing that the current system is immensely resistant to change.

The solution is very simple. Don't try and change it. It's a futile exercise and all the evidence shows that it doesn't work. Instead we can put our efforts into creating an alternative system. Such an alternative system can be based on 3 simple transitional principles. Firstly, we can "do it ourselves" rather than waiting for someone else, like politicians and business leaders, to do it. In every community everywhere, groups come together to address social issues in their own community. They can be small or large, but all share the characteristic of embodying somehow the principles of a different kind of society based on values of sharing, co-operation and goodwill. Whether it be a foodbank, a befriending group, a mental health support group or whatever doesn't matter. Rather it's the principle that somewhere someone has thought: "This need isn't being addressed. I can do something about it." Its where our true power lies. While the aforementioned examples are small-scale, it's not impossible to accomplish larger initiatives. There are multiple experiments throughout the world to create alternative money systems, local renewable energy grids, organic food production, waste recycling, even changes in the law... and much more. Huge amounts of money are available for these initiatives, whether it be crowdfunding, gifts, grant aid or the national lottery, the money is there waiting to be claimed and utilised. All that is needed is something that millions of people possess; imagination and the capacity to just make a start and see what happens. The multiplicity of such initiatives, a global movement of concerned citizens, has been described by author Paul Hawken in his book *Blessed Unrest* as "How the Largest Movement in the World Came into Being and Why No One Saw It Coming".

> *"Blessed Unrest tells the story of a worldwide movement that is largely unseen by politicians or the media. Hawken, an environmentalist and author, has spent more than a decade researching organizations dedicated to restoring the environment and fostering*

social justice. From billion-dollar nonprofits to single-person causes, these organizations collectively comprise the largest movement on earth. This is a movement that has no name, leader, or location, but is in every city, town, and culture. It is organizing from the bottom up and is emerging as an extraordinary and creative expression of people's needs worldwide."[39]

The second transition principle is to learn to work co-operatively in partnership with other people. Often the biggest obstacle to Hawken's largest movement in the world coming into being is the difficulty people have in working together. The establishment technique of "keep your mouth shut and do what you're told, or you won't get paid" doesn't work in these types of groups. Instead the freedom to do it ourselves can lead to an eruption of arguments and inter-personal hostility that erodes goodwill and ultimately the well-being & effectiveness of the group itself. If you've been involved yourself in these types of groups, you will inevitably have encountered that sort of stuff. Often, the assumed recourse is that we have to be "democratic". However, the inevitable result is that the voted upon will of the majority leads to a minority feeling alienated and rejected. A simple solution to this is to consider alternatives to democracy. Two alternatives come to mind. Sociocracy is a model

---

39. Quoted from
<https://www.goodreads.com/book/show/89998.Blessed_Unrest>

based on The Quakers (the Religious Society of Friends). The Quaker way is not to vote, as a way to find a collectively agreed way forward. Rather it is to discuss, listen carefully to each other, attune to a dimension of inner wisdom, keep cool, keep open and keep talking, until a way forward that all can support emerges and is obvious. It can take time, but it is time well spent.

The rapid rise of Extinction Rebellion exploded into public awareness with a never before seen output of actions, characterised by extraordinary levels of imagination, creativity, impact, individual commitment and organisational integrity; all within a short time-span, of just a few months from inception to coherent planet-wide expression. The scope of the group´s purpose offers one explanation for this, the way that it has resonated within the hearts & minds of intelligent people of goodwill another. However, of much greater significance is its adoption and demonstration of a new model of organisation structure: Holacracy. The idea was originally developed by Brian Robertson, a software entrepreneur, around 2007, in an endeavour to create greater autonomy, purpose-orientation, rapid decision-making, and evolution within his company. At its core are 3 guiding principles, that can be adopted, amended or adapted by any organisation or group. Firstly the principle of "devolved autonomy", where individuals/small groupings are encouraged and allowed to develop their own unique response to the

PURPOSE of the organisation, rather than being managed & limited by the traditional hierarchical structure of that organisation. This in turn leads to the 2nd holacracy principle of "innovative meeting practices", designed for rapid execution and creative expression, rather than time & energy consuming debates, discussions and decision making attempts. Many such techniques already exist and have been widely adopted, notably by Extinction Rebellion to develop a model for how a Citizen´s Assembly might effectively function. Both of these principles demand and also naturally lead to the 3rd principle of an "evolving organisational structure". Evolution & Diversity are natural principles throughout all of nature, whereas organisations can sometimes be hampered in their evolution by a fixed and inflexible structure. In such cases, the creative potential of the organisation is severely hampered by a focus on maintaining and following the existing structure rather than allowing it to naturally change & develop, driven by the creative diversity of the individuals comprising it.

Both these new models of collective decision making are examples of "system change" and naturally lead to our third transitional principle. The current global society is a direct and truthful expression of who we, as humans, are. Or at least what we think we are, leading to how we behave. This world as we know it, established during the last great transition of the 18th century Industrial

Revolution, is based on a number of core beliefs, the principal one being that each of us is a separate self-contained entity; separate from everything outside of the boundary of the physical body, separate from other human beings against whom we must protect ourselves, and separate from nature, which exists for us to use and exploit in any way that seems to help us feel good about ourselves, irrespective of the consequences. This is a narrative, paradigm, or "story in the mind" that many people subscribe to. In simplistic and blunt terms, the multiple crises of the modern world have a single cause; separative human consciousness. To make a massive generalisation, we are mainly talking about the consciousness of MEN. Women, on the other hand, with a natural and biological inclination towards the nurturing of life, collectively embody many of the human qualities needed for the new transition. The progressive liberation of the female psyche occurring throughout the 20th century is a significant development in the growing momentum towards a transition into sustainability.

How can we establish a new form of consciousness more closely aligned with the non-separative truths enunciated both by recent science and also new developments in psychological, social and ecological awareness? For most people, the answer to the question "who are you?" will probably elicit a response based around what you do, what your attitudes & beliefs are, what you feel in different situations, what your values are, what views you have, what tribe you identify with etc.. However, look very closely at yourself as you are in this moment and ask yourself "who am I?" You may observe a whole host of sensations, thoughts and feelings arising. For every single one of these assumed identities, you can be aware of them. Therefore, are you the thought feeling or sensation itself... or that which is aware of them? Look even closer. In the midst of this endless torrent of thinking and feeling, you may notice that there is always a peaceful watcher & awareness of these things arising; alert, silent, detached, intelligent, without boundaries, substance or spatial location. You are that. For some people, potentially all people, a close examination of the nature of this reality, has been known to result in a collapse of the sense of being a separate someone and a rebirth into a more universal expanded sense of consciousness.

To go back to the beginning of this book, the various major transitions listed can be likened to the growth and development of a child and young person. The first transition, the use of simple technologies, is similar to the young child beginning to reach out towards its toys. The development of language, the naming of things and the first steps into abstract and conceptual thinking, occur within all young children; a significant step in development. The agricultural transition has echoes of the young child beginning to look after itself; to wash, dress and use the toilet. The birth of civilisation has the adolescent beginning to step out into the world and find its way around, while the period of colonisation has parallels to the young person beginning to flex its muscles in the world and assert its own unique identity. Finally, the industrial revolution heralds a period of self-centred growth; powerful, assertive but without a clearly defined moral & ethical compass, beyond peer approval and magnification of self.

That ethical dimension comes later. It's called growing up and becoming a responsible adult. Ancient cultures, and modern indigenous cultures, mark this as a special moment in the individual life, often characterised by ritual events and involving some sort of trial or difficult challenge. As a human society, that's precisely where we are now. We are faced with an enormous challenge and our future well-being, indeed survival, depends on being able to successfully negotiate that challenge. For the ancients, the meeting of the challenge was not just a symbolic event, but rather an initiation of the person into taking their rightful and hard-earned place within the community. It could be that our "rightful place" within the planetary life community is that of a good idea; albeit an unsuccessful experiment that's gone tragically wrong, but, hey ho, life will learn from the experiment and try again. However, it could equally be that our rightful place is that of a wise presence, consciously embodying a loving planetary consciousness to create a society that successfully serves human need, engaged in a cooperative endeavour with other life forms to further the hidden aims of evolution; the shining forth into the universe of this "jewel of the cosmos".

It's got to be one or the other.

What's your choice?

Further Information

www.globaltransition.co.uk

Published by

www.kscreativearts.co.uk/#publishing

Published in Ingol, Preston, Lancashire, UK